"*The Substance of Our Faith* is a pastoral and church-leadership gem, illuminating the transformative power of historical d̶ our faith today. It invites church leaders to embrace the ̶ ̶it, cherish the authority of Scripture and trad̶ and connection with the saints, as t̶ wisdom and grace."

—**Laurent Mb̶** ̶an Church
of Rwanda an̶ ̶iocese; chairman
̶glican Future Conference)

"This book excels in two aspe̶ ̶̶, it stands out in terms of its structured approach, demonstrating a keen dedication to understanding the history of Christian doctrine correctly. The range of materials presented is extensive, encompassing Protestantism, Eastern Orthodoxy, and Roman Catholicism. Second, it considers a perspective on the universal church and the practical aspects of an individual's faith when seeking to understand the history of Christian doctrine. Sweeney's proposal to understand the history of Christian doctrine within the context of 'one church, with the church, and beneath the church' resonates as the voice of the Lord in an age marked by division, much like today. I strongly recommend giving it a read!"

—**Nam Joon Kim**, author of *Busy for Self, Lazy for God*; senior pastor
of Yullin Church, South Korea

"In an era of specialization (and overspecialization?), this book takes us back to the general scholarship practiced in earlier eras that is sorely lacking today. Written to address those Christians who are suspicious of doctrine as something that only divides, *The Substance of Our Faith* is aimed primarily at 'those who want to teach in the churches across time and space.' Deeply committed to a 'traditional and global' Christianity, Sweeney advocates convincingly for a Christianity that is best 'explained with the whole counsel of God—not the whole counsel of God as imparted in the West, but the whole counsel of God as conveyed by the whole people of God, past and present.' In particular, Sweeney's willingness to foray into the neglected Eastern fathers and explore patristics beyond Augustine is a welcome relief. Sweeney's work is a useful textbook on the development of doctrine, authority, and mission in the global church."

—**Rev. Fr. Gregory Edwards**, St. Vladimir's Orthodox
Theological Seminary

"Sweeney loves Christian truth. An expert historian of Protestant Christianity, Sweeney has a keen sense for global currents of faith. He is also a man of Scripture, which he discovers reflected in the creeds of those who have gone before us. In this book, Sweeney takes up the nature of doctrinal 'development' as understood by Christians from diverse times and confessional commitments. His winsomely Protestant proposal for an evangelical-catholic approach—normed by Scripture but pliable, interculturally engaged, and open-ended—will foster ecumenical conversation among all those who follow the Lord Jesus."

—**Matthew Levering**, Mundelein Seminary

"This book is vintage Sweeney—brimming with wisdom, refreshing in its passion for biblical orthodoxy, and rooted in a deep love for the church. Sweeney has much to teach us from key thinkers and episodes in the church across time and space. But most of all, he will restore your faith in the glorious future of Christ's bride. I cannot recommend this insightful book highly enough!"

—**Hans Madueme**, Covenant College

"Sweeney makes a deeply persuasive plea for Christians, whether in the pews or in the academy, to attend to the full breadth and depth of the history of Christian doctrine—across time, space, and ecclesial boundaries. But this wise, measured, and beautifully written book does more than make a theoretical case. Sweeney illustrates history of and for the church at its best and gives his readers the background and key concepts they need to join in on the grand adventure."

—**Han-luen Kantzer Komline**, Western Theological Seminary, Holland, Michigan

"The current volume is the first of two in which Sweeney endeavors to answer such questions as, How do we understand the church being holy, catholic, and apostolic? and What unites all churches in the world, whether those in the past, or those in the present with diverse backgrounds? In this book, Sweeney provides a lucid survey of the development of Christian doctrine. This much-needed study will be beneficial to God's people, particularly in this day and age in which doctrine becomes seemingly obsolete."

—**Aihe (Luke) Zheng**, International Chinese Biblical Seminary in Europe

"Driven by learning and devotion put in service to good history and theology, Sweeney offers here a convincing prologue to his forthcoming global history of Christian doctrine. He engages discerningly with relevant currents in contemporary theology to make the case for the possibility and necessity of global history today. The book treats a wide range of movements and theologians, emphasizing the catholicity of the faith across space and time. Readers will appreciate his open ecumenical posture and even-handed treatment of the teachings of the divided churches. Sweeney speaks convincingly across confessional lines. This is truly a book for all Christians!"

—**Mickey L. Mattox**, Hillsdale College

THE SUBSTANCE
of OUR FAITH

THE SUBSTANCE of OUR FAITH

Foundations *for the* History *of* Christian Doctrine

DOUGLAS A. SWEENEY

Ⅱᗷ
Baker Academic
a division of Baker Publishing Group
Grand Rapids, Michigan

© 2023 by Douglas A. Sweeney

Published by Baker Academic
a division of Baker Publishing Group
Grand Rapids, Michigan
www.bakeracademic.com

Printed in the United States of America

Library of Congress Cataloging in Publication Control Number: 2023014298

ISBN 978-0-8010-4846-3 (paperback)
ISBN 978-1-5409-6736-7 (casebound)
ISBN 978-1-4934-4467-0 (ebook)

Baker Publishing Group publications use paper produced from sustainable forestry practices and post-consumer waste whenever possible.

23   24   25   26   27   28   29   7   6   5   4   3   2   1

To Kevin and Sylvie Vanhoozer,
cherished friends and fellow disciples:

Ἡ φιλαδελφία μενέτω.

The gifts he gave were that some would be apostles, some prophets, some evangelists, some pastors and teachers, to equip the saints for the work of ministry, for building up the body of Christ, until all of us come to the unity of the faith and of the knowledge of the Son of God, to maturity, to the measure of the full stature of Christ. We must no longer be children, tossed to and fro and blown about by every wind of doctrine, by people's trickery, by their craftiness in deceitful scheming. But speaking the truth in love, we must grow up in every way into him who is the head, into Christ, from whom the whole body, joined and knitted together by every ligament with which it is equipped, as each part is working properly, promotes the body's growth in building itself up in love.

—Ephesians 4:11–16

Above all, clothe yourselves with love, which binds everything together in perfect harmony. And let the peace of Christ rule in your hearts, to which indeed you were called in the one body. And be thankful. Let the word of Christ dwell in you richly; teach and admonish one another in all wisdom; and with gratitude in your hearts sing psalms, hymns, and spiritual songs to God. And whatever you do, in word or deed, do everything in the name of the Lord Jesus, giving thanks to God the Father through him.

—Colossians 3:14–17

Then I saw a new heaven and a new earth; for the first heaven and the first earth had passed away, and the sea was no more. And I saw the holy city, the new Jerusalem, coming down out of heaven from God, prepared as a bride adorned for her husband. . . .

I saw no temple in the city, for its temple is the Lord God the Almighty and the Lamb. And the city has no need of sun or moon to shine on it, for the glory of God is its light, and its lamp is the Lamb. The nations will walk by its light, and the kings of the earth will bring their glory into it. Its gates will never be shut by day—and there will be no night there. People will bring into it the glory and the honour of the nations. But nothing unclean will enter it, nor anyone who practises abomination or falsehood, but only those who are written in the Lamb's book of life.

—Revelation 21:1–2, 22–27

CONTENTS

Preface

Only a tiny percentage of church adherents today understand very much about the substance of their faith. We profess to be spiritual. We say we love God and try our best to love others. But we know precious little *about* God, the Bible, the beliefs and practices of faraway Christians, or even those held dear by our own denominations. It is hard to love people we do not know well. We would not claim to love close friends we ignore. Christianity is often rife with acrimony and fractiousness. Our professions of love, then, to God and our neighbors have all too often rung hollow.

Doctrine is central to Christian discipleship. In the Greek New Testament, a disciple (μαθητής) is said to be a follower of Jesus who *learns* what he says and puts it into practice, becoming more like him in the process. Some Christians today are active in "discipleship," at least from time to time. They talk about their Christian lives in small-group settings, enabling one another to persevere in faith. But too little of this talk helps them get to know the Lord. Too many Christian leaders think that doctrine, in fact, turns "disciples" away, suppressing their desire to participate in church. They believe that the faith spreads best when presented as a minimal reliance on Jesus' death for sin and a grateful, if tranquil, tolerance and kindness. The knowledge and the love of God and neighbor, however, are meant to coincide, informing one another, not competing for attention. And most of what passes for discipleship today leaves its subjects in need of much more "solid food" (Heb. 5:11–14).[1] It impoverishes the church. It stunts the body of Christ. It contributes to the "juvenilization" of Christian faith and practice.[2] It impedes Christian love.

This book is the first of what will be two volumes on the substance of the faith. The project as a whole is designed to help readers come to understand God and his will for their lives, growing "to maturity," as Saint Paul urged, "to the measure of the full stature of Christ" (Eph. 4:13). The future volume will be much longer than this first one. It will narrate the history of the teaching of our churches all around the world, from the late first century to the twenty-first century (a daunting task indeed). This first book, though, has a rather different aim. It will survey a wide range of prefatory issues that accompany the study and application of this history: the role of God's Spirit in guiding our instruction; the authority of Scripture, creeds and confessions, traditions and instructors approved by the churches in clarifying what the Spirit wants from disciples; recognition of the global composition of the church and the difference this should make in the way we teach the faithful everywhere today; the debates about the nature, purposes, and changes in our doctrine over time; the modern reconception

1. After much deliberation, I have decided to use the Anglicised Edition of the New Revised Standard Version (NRSV) when citing the Bible in English. Its translation committee included scholars from all three branches of the worldwide Christian church (Orthodox, Catholic, and Protestant). It has since been approved for use in more denominations than any other English Bible (including thirty-three Protestant churches and the American and Canadian conferences of Catholic bishops). Though a Protestant myself, I employ the Catholic edition of the NRSV where it differs from the Protestant (such as in Esther and Daniel, or when quoting from the "Apocrypha," where both Catholics and Orthodox prefer to follow the canon of the Greek Old Testament, known as the Septuagint, rather than the Jewish/Hebrew Bible). If/when citing 1 Esdras, the Prayer of Manasseh, Psalm 151, or 3 Maccabees (deemed canonical by the Greek and Slavonic Orthodox, the latter of whose Bibles also include 2 Esdras), I will rely upon the NRSV Common Bible. If/when quoting from material found only in the canons of the Oriental Orthodox (i.e., the Syriac, Armenian, Ethiopian/Tewahedo, Eritrean/Tewahedo, Coptic, and Indian/Malankara Orthodox church bodies)—such as Jubilees, Psalms 152–55, 2 Baruch, Josippon, and the two Epistles of Clement—I will resort to a medley of modern English translations, as these canons vary greatly and we lack a common Oriental Orthodox Bible.

2. Thomas E. Bergler, *The Juvenilization of American Christianity* (Grand Rapids: Eerdmans, 2012).

of the notion, value, and force of tradition in contemporary teaching; and the chronic disagreements over whether and how best to use history—tradition—in the making of disciples, forming them in fellowship with all of God's family. This project takes for granted that doctrine is important, or should be important, to everyday people and highlights the ways in which different kinds of Christians have attended to the task of conveying it to others—in a global, orthodox, and edifying manner.

This book has four main chapters. The first zooms in on the sending of the Spirit and rise of Christian doctrine during early church history, exploring debates among Christians through the ages on the relative authority of Scripture, tradition, and leaders of the churches in handing on the faith. Chapter 2 treats the challenges of writing a global history of Christian faith and practice. It investigates the rise of what we call "the global south" in modern church history and shows that the Christian church has always been global, or at least international. It anticipates the aim of the longer, future volume to teach Christian faith across both time and space by accounting for the views of believers in the past *and* our kindred in Christ in other parts of the world as we inculcate the faith in our own backyards. Chapter 3 answers questions about the origins, nature, and purposes of doctrine and engages the history of learned conversation on adjudicating rival doctrinal developments. The fourth and final chapter limns the ways in which teachers employ the tradition in their ministries today, offering advice about using church history in Christian catechesis moving forward.

As I specify below, I define Christian doctrine as a form of church teaching intended for the shaping of daily faith and practice. While I deal at some length in this project with the work of academic theologians, I do so in view of its effect on church teaching (not independent research or academic trends). "Doctrine" means teaching. It is given by the Lord to assist the people of God. It is inculcated best in communion with the saints—past and present, at home and around the world.

I will major, in what follows, on the authorized teachings of the mainstream churches, paying most attention to the doctrines conveyed across multiple traditions of the worldwide church. I am writing this project for Christians everywhere—Orthodox, Catholic, Protestant, and other—but speaking most directly to Christians who "mean it," who find doctrine important and want to get it right, who hold ecumenism, orthodoxy, and real catholicity in high esteem, who desire to mature and help others mature as they hand on the faith. I will not devote as much time to topics stressed in only one of the branches of the global family of God (the priority of Saint John Chrysostom's liturgy, papal infallibility, glossolalia as evidence of Spirit baptism) as to topics taught by all (the nature of the church, the triunity of God, the way of salvation, the love of God and neighbor in the lives of believers). I will take due pains to describe and interpret the doctrinal divergences between our traditions but will foreground teachings most Christians share in common.

I take this approach because I truly believe, in the words of the creed, that we share one, holy, catholic, and apostolic church. In the mercy of God, all Christians everywhere "are a chosen race, a royal priesthood, a holy nation, God's own people, in order that you may proclaim the mighty acts of him who called you out of darkness into his marvellous light" (1 Pet. 2:9). In the pages that follow, I will highlight our ethnic and doctrinal diversity. But because I believe that real followers of Jesus compose one family, my burden in this project is to narrate the story of the history of doctrine as a tragicomic tale of our reconciled diversity. In the book of Revelation, "the kings of the earth" are said to "bring their glory" to the new Jerusalem. "People will bring into it the glory and the honour of the nations," we read. This cultural display is not the endgame, however. As the nations assemble around the throne of God, their cultural treasures are presented to the Lord. Then all those "written in the Lamb's book of life" are enraptured—together, unselfconsciously, joyfully—in wonder, love, and praise (Rev. 21:24–27). God's unity prevails.

⊖⊖⊖⊖

I refer in this project to "churches" and "Churches," "orthodoxy" and "Orthodoxy," "catholics" and "Catholics." I capitalize words like these only in proper nouns or when quoting from others. Thus churches in this project are groups of believers referred to in general (e.g., the churches of Asia), while Churches are particular, institutional bodies (e.g., the Roman Catholic Church). The orthodox are those who maintain views authorized within their traditions, while the Orthodox are members of Eastern Orthodox churches. Proponents of catholicism are those who prefer a comprehensive, international approach to the faith, while proponents of Catholicism are those who prefer views favored by bodies with Catholic in the name (usually Roman Catholic churches). These usages are common, and nearly unavoidable in books like this. Attention to their details may help some readers.

The global history of doctrine is immense in scale, impossible to trek without help from one's friends. I am grateful to mine for assistance of various kinds. Carl Beckwith, Gregory Edwards, John Hannah, Gerald Hiestand, Glenn Kreider, Matthew Levering, Scott Manetsch, Ken Minkema, Tom Oey, Craig Ott, David Pao, Tite Tiénou, Kevin Vanhoozer, and Lionel Young lent timely advice. Before COVID-19, Matthew Levering and his colleague Emery de Gaál, and Glenn Kreider and his president Mark M. Yarbrough, invited me for lectures in Mundelein and Dallas that helped me flesh out some material adapted for use in chapter 1.[3] Colby Brandt, Samuel Hagos, Bradley Hansen, and Theo Siu worked as research assistants, tracking down sources and engaging me in learned conversation as

3. This material was printed in these colleagues' publications. See Douglas A. Sweeney, "Ratzinger on Scripture, Tradition, and Church: An Evangelical Assessment," in *Joseph Ratzinger and the Healing of the Reformation-Era Divisions*, ed. Emery de Gaál and Matthew Levering (Steubenville, OH: Emmaus Academic Press, 2019); Sweeney, "Jesus's Promise of the Spirit and the Teaching of the Faith: From Kerygma to Catechesis," *Bibliotheca Sacra* 178 (January–March 2021): 3–13; Sweeney, "Creeds, Canons, Councils, and the Contest over Tradition," *Bibliotheca Sacra* 178 (April–June 2021): 131–42; two further installments are forthcoming from *Bibliotheca Sacra*. Used by permission.

I wrote. Luke Buttram and Caroline Bass compiled the index. Most importantly of all, David Kirkpatrick, David Kling, David Luy, and Hans Madueme worked through the manuscript, making thoughtful suggestions, pointing out problems, and offering encouragement. My work is much better for their friendship.

I will be forever grateful to my brothers and sisters in the global family of God for the ways in which many of them have shaped my faith and practice, enriching my life. I extend special thanks, though, to Kevin and Sylvie Vanhoozer, the dearest of friends. I dedicate this work to them with love and great joy in the fellowship we share.

1

Jesus' Promise of the Spirit

If you love me, you will keep my commandments. And I will ask the Father, and he will give you another Advocate, to be with you forever. This is the Spirit of truth, whom the world cannot receive, because it neither sees him nor knows him. You know him, because he abides with you, and he will be in you.

... The Advocate, the Holy Spirit, whom the Father will send in my name, will teach you everything, and remind you of all that I have said to you. ...

... I tell you the truth: it is to your advantage that I go away, for if I do not go away, the Advocate will not come to you; but if I go, I will send him to you. ...

I still have many things to say to you, but you cannot bear them now. When the Spirit of truth comes, he will guide you into all the truth; for he will not speak on his own, but will speak whatever he hears, and he will declare to you the things that are to come. He will glorify me, because he will take what is mine and declare it to you.

—John 14:15–17, 26; 16:7, 12–14

There would be no history of doctrine if Jesus had not promised the Spirit to disciples in the upper room before his crucifixion.[1] Or, at least, the history of doctrine would have proven far poorer. Still frightened and confused, the apostles needed help understanding and believing—let alone handing on—what the master had been teaching. They had lived with their rabbi for about three years. Still, they failed to comprehend much of what the Lord had said. They abandoned him, in fact, when the going got tough. One sold him out to members of the Jewish Sanhedrin who sought to have him killed. Even the boldest of the group, named the "rock" by Jesus (Πέτρος in Greek; Matt. 16:18), denied him three times. Jesus seems to have foreseen their bewilderment and weakness. In keeping with an inner-trinitarian arrangement, he assured them that the Spirit would soon come alongside them, abide with them, speak to them, reignite their faithfulness, and help them sort things out.

Less than two months later, this promise was fulfilled. On the day of Pentecost, or Jewish Festival of Weeks (*Shavuot*), the disciples "were . . . together in one place," wrote Luke, a close associate of Paul who had investigated the sources of his story carefully (Luke 1:1–4; Acts 1:1–5). "And suddenly from heaven there came a sound like the rush of a violent wind, and it filled the entire house where they were sitting. Divided tongues, as of fire, appeared among them, and a tongue rested on each of them. All of them were filled with the Holy Spirit and began to speak in other languages, as the Spirit gave them ability" (Acts 2:2–4). Jews "from every nation" (2:5) had assembled in Jerusalem to keep *Shavuot* (in honor of the harvest and, according to tradition, to commemorate the giving of the law on Mount Sinai). Astounded by this miracle, "each one heard them speaking in the native language of each" (2:6). Peter addressed the throng, now behaving

---

1. New Testament scholars disagree about where Jesus and the apostles were by John 16. At the end of John 14, Jesus said to the apostles, "Rise, let us be on our way." But not until 18:1, "after Jesus had spoken these words" (presumably, the words that had begun in the upper room), did they go "out" and cross the Kidron Valley to the garden of Gethsemane. Many think it likely that they stayed in the upper room throughout the whole "upper room discourse" (John 13–17).

like the rock Jesus told him he would be. Reminding everyone who listened of the prophecy of Joel ("Then afterwards I will pour out my spirit on all flesh; your sons and your daughters shall prophesy," etc.; Joel 2:28), he testified that Jesus had arisen from the dead, ascended to the Father, and effected what the prophet had foretold long ago—and what Jesus had predicted only seven weeks ago. "Being therefore exalted at the right hand of God," Peter preached, Jesus, the Messiah, "has poured out this that you . . . see and hear" today (Acts 2:33).

For nearly two millennia, Christian leaders have debated the importance of the sending of the Spirit for their ministries, especially the ministry of handing on the faith. Just what did Jesus mean when he promised that the Spirit would guide us "into all the truth" (John 16:13), many of them have queried? How much of "all the truth" has been codified in Scripture? How much was revealed after the closing of the canon? Does the Spirit still speak outside the leaves of Scripture? If so, how are we to understand what he is saying?

Modern liberals have suggested that the Spirit still guides us into truths not seen in either Scripture or tradition, primarily by inspiring the development and spread of our most charitable and liberating global cultural values. Conservative, or "old-school," Protestants demur, saying Jesus sent the Spirit not to shape secular values but to guide the first disciples as they wrote the New Testament. With the founding of the church and the closing of the canon, they contend, God's Spirit stopped sharing new truths and, instead, helped Christians understand what was written. Roman Catholics, Eastern Orthodox,[2] and most other Christians stand somewhere in the middle of these first two positions. Roman Catholics say the Spirit still leads us into truths not codified before, but only through the office

2. The Eastern Orthodox Church is more technically, though far less commonly, referred to as the Orthodox Catholic Church. It is also known simply as the Orthodox Church. I will use all three of these names in what follows, partly to distinguish these Christians from Roman Catholics and partly to make clear that the Orthodox Church is found outside the "East" as well.

of the Catholic magisterium (composed of all the bishops in communion with the pope). The Orthodox affirm that the Spirit led the early church fathers in their work, superintending the results of the first seven, so-called ecumenical councils, and continues to inspire local councils in their work in a manner that yields teaching less authoritative than that of the ancient church fathers.[3] Pentecostals are convinced that the Spirit has been poured out again in recent days (i.e., the "last days," inaugurated in the nineteenth century, at least according to most), mainly to enable us to live according to Scripture and to hasten Christ's return with evangelistic power. And most other Protestants are somewhat less certain what to make of the leading of the Spirit in the present. The majority believe that the Spirit still speaks but hesitate to separate that speech from the Scriptures. Word and Spirit work together, these Protestants aver. When the Spirit speaks now, he appropriates the Word, helping those with ears to hear to understand, obey, and make use of the Bible and the best of church history to improvise responses to uniquely modern questions.

I will flesh these positions out further in what follows. For now, what matters is that nearly all Christians owe the teachings of their churches to the sending of the Spirit. He steered the first Christians after Jesus' resurrection, ascension, and session at the Father's right hand. He inspired the disciples as they wrote the New Testament. And he helped the church fathers—and later doctors of the church—as they handed on the faith then "entrusted to the saints" (Jude 3). In the rest of this chapter, I will explore this history and introduce readers to debates that attend the task of sorting out the Spirit's work in

3. In 2016, a "Holy and Great Council of the Orthodox Church" was convened on the isle of Crete. Its organizers planned a "Pan-Orthodox" gathering, far more authoritative than regional conventions. It was led by the Patriarch Bartholomew I, archbishop of the ancient city of Constantinople (present-day Istanbul), first among equals in the Orthodox episcopate. But as the meeting drew near, several Orthodox churches refused to attend (the Russians most importantly, but Antioch, Bulgaria, Georgia, and the church in America as well), undercutting its significance.

Scripture and tradition. We will focus most frequently on two main questions: In what ways has the Spirit led us into all the truth? And what is the relative authority of Scripture, tradition, and the leaders of our churches in clarifying what the Spirit wants from disciples?

Lest we lose ourselves in intramural controversy, let's remember that the Spirit is still at work in the world today and wants to help us make good use of the history of our faith. As most faithful Christian teachers have affirmed over the centuries, the Spirit grants cognitive and ethical advantages to those who seek to grow in the practice of the faith—even two thousand years after the pouring out at Pentecost (1 Cor. 2). So the surest way forward for believers in the present is to study Christian doctrine, try to walk with the Spirit, and encircle oneself with other like-minded disciples—past and present, near and far—interpreting one's learning in communion with the saints and checking one's perspective against the teaching of their churches, thereby grounding one's practice in the ripest fruit of the Spirit's work in Scripture, tradition, and the worldwide family of God. God's Word is too important to engage in isolation, the faithful too finite (not to mention hard-hearted) to apply it on our own. We "see in a mirror, dimly" (1 Cor. 13:12), limited by personal and sociocultural blinders. So we need the Lord's help to improve on what we learn. "No one comprehends" the things of God except God's Spirit, but "those who are spiritual discern all things" (2:11, 15).

Kerygma, Rules of Faith, Canons of Scripture, and the Spirit

Christians have long disagreed about the optimal relationship of Scripture, tradition, and discernment of the Spirit in the teaching of the church, a debate to appear in more detail in chapter 3. But honesty requires that all parties to the controversy assent to something like the following history lying behind it, a history of the impact of primitive proclamation of the gospel of Jesus Christ (κήρυγμα), the unwritten traditions of the Lord's own apostles (pertaining, some claim, to institutions like fasting, prayer, sacraments, devotion to the saints and their images, virginity, and more), ancient worship (*lex orandi*), rules of faith (*regulis fidei*), creeds and councils, canons of Scripture, and the leading of the Spirit in the pedagogical ministries of ecumenical churches (the churches that intend to be "catholic," that is, meaning universal and orthodox).

The biblical materials spotlight consistently the word of the Lord as revealed through Christ, his prophets, and his apostles as the ultimate authority for guiding God's people. Relatedly, they highlight "the sacred writings" themselves, given by inspiration of God, which "are able to instruct you," as Paul wrote Timothy, "for salvation through faith in Christ Jesus" (2 Tim. 3:15–16). Traditions not given by direct inspiration simply pale by comparison, when not condemned for sinfulness and often even hypocrisy. As Jesus asked the Pharisees and scribes who condemned his disciples for transgressing the traditions of the elders, "Why do you break the commandment of God for the sake of your tradition? . . . You make void the word of God. You hypocrites!" he chided. "Isaiah prophesied rightly about you when he said: 'This people honours me with their lips, but their hearts are far from me; in vain do they worship me, teaching human precepts as doctrines" (Matt. 15:1–9; Isa. 29:13). The Lord and his prophets said the like many times, calling people to repent of their glib devotion to convention and submit to the word of God itself.

But neither Christ nor his witnesses eschewed all tradition. Tradition understood as *paradosis* (παράδοσις), in fact—as handing on the Word, teaching and doing what it says—was advocated repeatedly throughout the Hebrew Scriptures and early Christian history. The Old Testament brims with admonition from the Lord to disseminate his teachings. "Recite them to your children," God commanded through Moses after giving the Shema ("Hear, O Israel," etc.), "and talk about them when you are at home and when you are away, when you lie down and when you rise. Bind them as a sign on your hand, fix them as an emblem on your forehead, and write them on the doorposts of your house and on your gates" (Deut. 6:7–9). And early Christian leaders spoke frequently of guarding and imparting the deposit of the faith they received: both Old Testament teaching and the kerygmatic witness and tuition of the apostles. Shortly after the resurrection and before his ascension, Jesus told the Eleven to "make disciples of all nations, . . . teaching them to obey everything that I have commanded you" (Matt. 28:18–20). So during and after Pentecost, they did just that. Soon thousands of believers "devoted themselves" to the apostles' "teaching . . . , to the breaking of bread and the prayers" (Acts 2:42).

The New Testament writings bleed costly Christian witness to the efforts of disciples to perpetuate the pattern of instruction they received. From the martyr Stephen's speech to the Jewish Sanhedrin (Acts 7) through the treacherous peregrinations of the ministry of Paul to the epistolary labors of the New Testament authors—often undertaken from prison—and the pedagogical programs that were built upon their teaching (1 Cor. 3:10), they preserved and transmitted the tradition they possessed. "Timothy, guard what has been entrusted to you," Paul urged his charge. "Hold to the standard of sound teaching. . . . Guard the good treasure entrusted to you, with the help of the Holy Spirit." And "what you have heard from me," he appended programmatically, "entrust to faithful people who will be able to teach others" (1 Tim. 6:20; 2 Tim. 1:13–14; 2:2). "Contend for the faith," pleaded Jude the brother of James, "that was once for all entrusted to the saints" by the apostles (Jude 3). For as Irenaeus echoed in his work *Against Heresies* (ca. 175–85), "the Church has received from the apostles and imparted" the one and "only true and life-giving faith."[4] And as Tertullian would stress in *Prescription against Heretics* (ca. 200), nothing was withheld from this transmission process. Everything needed for salvation was included, and troublemakers boasting

4. Irenaeus, *Adversus haereses*, 3.preface; trans. at New Advent, http://www.newadvent.org /fathers/0103.htm.

secret teaching should be stopped lest they turn some aside from the riches of the Lord.[5]

This strenuous commitment to protect and promote the instruction of the apostles stemmed in part from the importance of the Scriptures in the synagogues. Jews had long valorized the teaching of the Word. But it also came from Christian trust that Jesus' resurrected life and teaching brought salvation. "I should remind you, brother and sisters," Paul wrote the Corinthians,

> of the good news that I proclaimed to you, which you in turn received, in which also you stand, through which also you are being saved, if you hold firmly to the message that I proclaimed to you. . . .
>
> For I handed on to you as of first importance what I in turn had received: that Christ died for our sins in accordance with the scriptures, and that he was buried, and that he was raised on the third day in accordance with the scriptures, and that he appeared to Cephas, then to the twelve. Then he appeared to more than five hundred brothers and sisters at one time, most of whom are still alive, though some have died. Then he appeared to James, then to all the apostles. (1 Cor. 15:1–7)

Instruction about Jesus' resurrection changed the world. Christian doctrine was life and death, and the contest surrounding it demanded close attention. Paul went on to warn,

> If Christ has not been raised, then our proclamation has been in vain and your faith has been in vain. We are even found to be misrepresenting God, because we testified of God that he raised Christ. . . . If Christ has not been raised, your faith is futile and you are still in your sins. Then those also who have died in Christ have perished. If for this life only we have hoped in Christ, we are of all people most to be pitied. (15:14–19)

A great deal depended on early Christian *paradosis*.

5. Tertullian, *De praescriptione haereticorum* 25–26.

The apostles also inculcated unwritten traditions, though we lack the means to verify the ones taught by Jesus and adjudicate rival Christian claims about their value. As explained in John's Gospel, the Savior did many things witnessed by disciples that were not written down. If all of them were registered, "the world itself could not contain the books that would be written" (John 20:30; 21:25). And Jesus told the Twelve that when the Holy Spirit came, he would "guide [them] into all the truth" (16:13), helping them remember things never put to writing and, presumably, revealing even more from the Lord. This promise came true at the Council of Jerusalem, whose verdict in the case of the gentile Christians "seemed good to the . . . Spirit and to us," wrote Luke (Acts 15:28). It resulted in the writing of the New Testament books. And it yielded oral teaching bearing apostolic warrant. Paul told the Thessalonians, "Stand firm and hold fast to the traditions that you were taught by us, either by word of mouth or by our letter" (2 Thess. 2:15). He encouraged those at Corinth just a few years later, "I commend you because you . . . maintain the traditions just as I handed them on to you" (1 Cor. 11:2).

In early church history, episcopal supervision of the church's faith and practice gained prominence as surety for apostolic orthodoxy—written and unwritten. Heresy emerged, the primal Christian witness needed careful transmission, and the worship of the faithful demanded sound guidance. Oral teaching found its way into everyday piety through prayers to the saints, eucharistic rites, and more—all supervised closely by the bishops and their aides. These never formed the cornerstone of any cardinal doctrine. But they did play a role in the teaching of the churches as the law of supplication—in worship and devotion—turned rule for belief (*lex orandi, lex credendi*). According to the testimony of Basil of Caesarea (ca. 375), "Of the beliefs and practices whether generally accepted or publicly enjoined which are preserved in the Church some we possess derived from written teaching; others we have received delivered to us in a mystery by the tradition of the apostles; and both of these in relation to true religion have the same force. And these no one will gainsay—no one, at all events, who is even moderately versed in the institutions of the Church."[6] And in the words of an episcopal admonition issued shortly after the Council of Ephesus (431), "Let us be mindful of the sacraments of priestly public prayer, which handed down by the Apostles are uniformly celebrated in the whole world and in every Catholic Church, in order that the law of supplication may support the law of believing."[7]

These ecclesiastical trends took shape in relation to several short, pithy summaries of kerygmatic faith that were employed as rules of faith and the interpretation of Scripture. The apostles wrote the most important kerygmatic statements. A few were simple sketches of the doctrine of the Trinity (Matt. 28:19; 2 Cor. 13:13; Eph. 3:14–17; 1 Pet. 1:1–2). Others spoke of Christ in light of Old Testament Scripture, or of Father, Son, and Spirit in creation and redemption. Paul summarized in Romans what he called

> the gospel of God, which he promised beforehand through his prophets in the holy scriptures, the gospel concerning his Son, who was descended from David according to the flesh and was declared to be Son of God with power according to the spirit of holiness by resurrection from the dead, Jesus Christ our Lord, through whom we have received grace and apostleship to bring about the obedience of faith among all the Gentiles for the sake of his name. (Rom. 1:1–5)

6. Basil of Caesarea, *On the Holy Spirit* 27.66; trans. at New Advent, http://www.newadvent .org/fathers/3203.htm.

7. "The Catalog or the Authoritative Statements of the Past Bishops of the Holy See concerning the Grace of God," chap. 8 in Henry Denzinger, *The Sources of Catholic Dogma*, trans. Roy J. Deferrari (New York: Herder, 1957; previously published in Latin as *Enchiridion Symbolorum, definitionum et declarationum de rebus fidei et morum*, 13th ed. [Freiburg im Breisgau: Herder, 1954]), §139 (p. 56). Pope Pius IX, on December 20, 1928, in an apostolic constitution called *Divini Cultus*, attributed this statement to Pope Celestine I, noting the "intimate relationship between dogma and sacred liturgy, and likewise between Christian worship and the sanctification of the people." Denzinger suggested that the "Catalog" in which the statement appears was organized "at Rome by St. Prosper of Aquitaine . . . shortly after CELESTINE I, between 435 and 442, and, about the year 500 [seems] to have been recognized universally as the genuine doctrine of the Apostolic See" (p. 52, n. 4).

To the Philippians, he quoted an early creedal hymn of Christ,

> who, though he was in the form of God, did not regard equality with
> God as something to be exploited, but emptied himself, taking the
> form of a slave, being born in human likeness. And being found in
> human form, he humbled himself and became obedient to the point
> of death—even death on a cross. Therefore God also highly exalted
> him and gave him the name that is above every name, so that at the
> name of Jesus every knee should bend, in heaven and on earth and
> under the earth, and every tongue should confess that Jesus Christ is
> Lord, to the glory of God the Father. (Phil. 2:6–11)

To the Colossians, Paul made an even grander gospel summary:
God "has rescued us," he wrote,

> from the power of darkness and transferred us into the kingdom of his
> beloved Son, in whom we have redemption, the forgiveness of sins.
>   He is the image of the invisible God, the firstborn of all creation; for
> in him all things in heaven and on earth were created, things visible
> and invisible, whether thrones or dominions or rulers or powers—
> all things have been created through him and for him. He himself is
> before all things, and in him all things hold together. He is the head
> of the body, the church; he is the beginning, the firstborn from the
> dead, so that he might come to have first place in everything. For in
> him all the fullness of God was pleased to dwell, and through him
> God was pleased to reconcile to himself all things, whether on earth
> or in heaven, by making peace through the blood of his cross. (Col.
> 1:13–20)

Other apostles, too, published kerygmatic statements. Peter wrote
to "exiles" dispersed in Asia Minor that Christ

> suffered for sins once for all, the righteous for the unrighteous, in order
> to bring you to God. He was put to death in the flesh, but made alive

in the spirit, in which also he went and made a proclamation to the spirits in prison, who in former times did not obey, when God waited patiently in the days of Noah, during the building of the ark, in which a few, that is, eight people, were saved through water. And baptism, which this prefigured, now saves you—not as a removal of dirt from the body, but as an appeal to God for a good conscience, through the resurrection of Jesus Christ, who has gone into heaven and is at the right hand of God, with angels, authorities, and powers made subject to him. (1 Pet. 3:18–22)

And John assured Christians of the basics of the faith as an unstable mix of other teachings cluttered their minds nearly a generation later: "We declare to you what was from the beginning, what we have heard, what we have seen with our eyes, what we have looked at and touched with our hands"—namely,

God is light and in him there is no darkness at all. If we say that we have fellowship with him while we are walking in darkness, we lie and do not do what is true; but if we walk in the light as he himself is in the light, we have fellowship with one another, and the blood of Jesus his Son cleanses us from all sin. If we say that we have no sin, we deceive ourselves, and the truth is not in us. If we confess our sins, he who is faithful and just will forgive us our sins and cleanse us from all unrighteousness. (1 John 1:5–9)

As the church and the needs of its members grew apace, postapostolic leaders well versed in Christian teaching took the learning they received and adapted it for use in various liturgies, apologies, and catechetical aids. The ancient church orders represent their efforts well. They epitomized the faith for use in early Christian liturgies and codified the creed required of those seeking baptism. (A few of these orders boast an apostolic pedigree, though none bears a clear and free title to such a claim.) The earliest, the Didache (late first-century

Syria), contains only a brief sketch of trinitarian faith.[8] But the Apostolic Tradition (ca. 215), often attributed to the presbyter Hippolytus of Rome, lays out in more detail the faith of many early baptizands. "When the person being baptized goes down into the water," it says,

> he who baptizes him putting his hands on him shall say: "Do you believe in God, the Father Almighty?" And the person being baptized shall say: "I believe." Then holding his hand on his head, he shall baptize him once. And then he shall say: "Do you believe in Christ Jesus, the Son of God, who was born of the Holy Spirit and the Virgin Mary, and was crucified under Pontius Pilate, and was dead and buried, and rose again the third day, alive from the dead, and ascended into heaven, and sat down at the right hand of the Father, and will come to judge the living and the dead?" And when the person says: "I believe," he is baptized again.
>
> And again the deacon shall say: "Do you believe in the Holy Spirit, in the holy church, and in the resurrection of the body?" Then the person being baptized shall say: "I believe," and he is baptized a third time.[9]

Kerygmatic summaries led to laws of supplication, which, in turn, ruled early Christian faith, practice, and worship.

Early church fathers also published creedal summaries in apologetic texts. Most famously, Justin Martyr, whose *First Apology* (ca. 155–57) included several well-known creedal fragments, made a series of such statements in his *Dialogue with Trypho* (ca. 155–67), which would later reappear in the ecumenical creeds. He penned this, for example, in chapter 85:

> In the name of this very Son of God and first-begotten of all
>   creation,
> Who was born through the Virgin,

---

8. The Didache ["Teaching"] 7.1–4, in *Creeds & Confessions of Faith in the Christian Tradition*, 4 vols., ed. Jaroslav Pelikan and Valerie Hotchkiss (New Haven: Yale University Press, 2003; hereafter Pelikan and Hotchkiss), 1:42.

9. Apostolic Tradition 21.12–18, in Pelikan and Hotchkiss, 1:61.

And became a passible man,
And was crucified under Pontius Pilate by your people,
And died,
And rose again from the dead,
And ascended to heaven,
Every demon is exorcised, conquered, and subdued.[10]

Such patterns of instruction and belief recurred frequently.

With the conversion of the empire longer teaching aids appeared, which systematized the Christian faith for use among the swelling ranks of public catechumens. Cyril of Jerusalem promoted such productions. In his *Catechetical Lectures* (ca. 348), he exhorted younger Christians, "Attend closely to the catechisings, and though we should prolong our discourse, let not your mind be wearied out. . . . You have many enemies; take to you many darts. . . . The armour is ready, and most ready *the sword of the Spirit*: but [you] also must stretch forth your right hand with good resolution, that you may war the Lord's warfare, and overcome adverse powers, and become invincible against every heretical attempt."[11] Gregory of Nyssa's *Great Catechism* (ca. 385) cultivated a similar perspective on the need for catechesis. "The presiding ministers of the 'mystery of godliness,'" it emphasized, "have need of a system in their instructions, in order that the Church may be replenished by the accession of such as should be saved, through the teaching of the word of Faith being brought home to the hearing of unbelievers."[12] Augustine wrote a treatise on the art of catechizing.[13] And these publications culminated in later, longer, even more

10. Justin Martyr, *Dialogus cum Tryphone* 85, as presented in Pelikan and Hotchkiss, 1:22–23; alternative trans. at New Advent, http://www.newadvent.org/fathers/01286.htm.

11. Cyril of Jerusalem, *Catecheses* (Κατηχήσεις), procatechesis [prologue] 10; trans. at New Advent, http://www.newadvent.org/fathers/310100.htm.

12. Gregory of Nyssa, *Oratio Catechetica* prologue; trans. at Wikisource, s.v. "Nicene and Post-Nicene Fathers: Series II/Volume V/Apologetic Works/The Great Catechism," https://en.wiki source.org/wiki/Nicene_and_Post-Nicene_Fathers:_Series_II/Volume_V/Apologetic_Work s/The_Great_Catechism.

13. Augustine, *De catechizandis rudibus* (ca. 400).

comprehensive compendia of Christian faith and practice by Theo-doret of Cyrus, John of Damascus, and others used by scholars and their teachers more than laity.[14]

Meanwhile, church leaders championed the ideal of orthodoxy, fighting to defend the deposit of the faith handed down by conserva-tives in mainstream churches as new sects and heterodox philosophies arose. Bishop Polycarp of Smyrna, who was martyred for his fortitude, cautioned the Philippians (ca. 110), "Whosoever perverts the oracles of the Lord to his own lusts, and says that there is neither a resurrec-tion nor a judgment," as some had done lately, "he is the first-born of Satan." Adding admonition to insult, he beckoned to the wayward to return "to the word which has been handed down to us from the be-ginning" of the church.[15] Irenaeus advocated using "rules" to guard the faith, simple aphoristic summaries of apostolic teaching over against which theological claims could be measured. He employed a "rule of truth" (*regula veritatis*) ten times in *Against Heresies* (ca. 175–85)[16] and a "rule of faith" (*regula fidei*) twice in *Proof of the Apostolic Preaching* (ca. 180).[17] Hippolytus of Rome did the same soon thereafter, wielding a doctrinal "rule of the truth" in *Refutation of All Heresies* (early third century).[18] And Tertullian, Novatian, Clement, Origen, and Cyprian also regulated orthodox theology with vigor, making a way for conciliar definitions of the faith in the fourth and fifth centuries.[19] Gregory of

---

14. Theodoret of Cyrus, *Hæreticarum fabularum compendium* (ca. 452), the five books of which are known collectively in English as *The Discernment of Falsehood and Truth*; John of Damascus, Πηγή Γνώσεως (*Pēgē Gnōseōs* [Fount of knowledge], ca. 740s), the most doctrinal part of which is called "The Orthodox Faith." Origen of Alexandria, *De principiis* (ca. 220s), is also a lengthy, early compendium of Christian faith and practice.

15. Polycarp, *To the Philippians* 7.1–2; trans. at New Advent, http://www.newadvent.org/fathers/0136.htm.

16. Irenaeus, *Adversus haereses*; trans. at New Advent, http://www.newadvent.org/fathers/0103.htm.

17. Irenaeus, *Proof* (Ἐπίδειξις) *of the Apostolic Preaching* 3, 6; trans. at Christian Classics Ethe-real Library, http://www.ccel.org/ccel/irenaeus/demonstr.iv.html.

18. Hippolytus, *Refutatio omnium haeresium* 10.1; trans. at New Advent, http://www.newadvent.org/fathers/0501.htm.

19. See, for example, Tertullian, *De praescriptione haereticorum* 13; Novatian, *De Trinitate* 1.9; Clement of Alexandria, *Stromata* 4.15; 6.15, 18; Origen, *De principiis* preface.2; Cyprian, *De unitate ecclesiae* 19.

Nyssa represented their rationale at the climax of the fourth-century trinitarian controversy. "It is enough for proof of our [doctrine]," he averred *Against Eunomius* (ca. 381), "that the tradition has come down to us from our fathers, handed on, like some inheritance, by succession from the apostles and the saints who came after them."[20]

These regulations culminated in full-blown creeds, some of which were published widely and one of which was used in both Eastern and Western churches. The best-known among them are the Old Roman Symbol and the "ecumenical" creeds: the poorly named Apostles' Creed, the Nicene Creed (or Niceno-Constantinopolitan Creed, received in East and West), and the Athanasian Creed. The first of these statements was the Old Roman Symbol, a baptismal creed of the Roman church that dates to the late second century. There are minor variations in the versions that survive, but the oldest reads as follows:

> I believe, therefore, in God Almighty and in Christ Jesus, his only-begotten Son, our Lord, who was born from the Holy Spirit and the Virgin Mary. Who was crucified under Pontius Pilate and buried, and on the third day rose from the dead. He ascended into the heavens and is seated at the right hand of the Father, whence he will come to judge the living and the dead. And [I believe] in the Holy Spirit, the holy church, the forgiveness of sins, the resurrection of the flesh, and life everlasting.[21]

As many will have recognized, these affirmations reverberated in most later creeds.

The next of these statements is the so-called Apostles' Creed, professed in many Western congregations most Sundays. Legend has it that the apostles wrote this document on Pentecost, each of them supplying one of its twelve sacred lines. But the creed is not cited

20. Gregory of Nyssa, *Contra Eunomium* 4.6; trans. at New Advent, http://www.newadvent.org/fathers/2901.htm.
21. Pelikan and Hotchkiss, 1:681–82.

till the late fourth century (at least not in extant documents), and its text first appears in an eighth-century handbook by Pirminius of Reichenau, a missionary monk. "I believe in God, the Father Almighty," it begins,

> Creator of heaven and earth. And in Jesus Christ, his only Son, our Lord, who was conceived of the Holy Spirit, born of the Virgin Mary, suffered under Pontius Pilate, was crucified, died, and was buried; he descended into hell. On the third day he rose from the dead; he ascended into heaven, sits at the right hand of God the Father Almighty. Thence he shall come to judge the living and the dead. I believe in the Holy Spirit, the holy catholic church, the communion of saints, the forgiveness of sins, the resurrection of the body, and the life everlasting. Amen.[22]

Now available in every major language in the world, it is even used occasionally by Orthodox thinkers. It has shaped Christian teaching like no other single source outside the Bible.

The Nicene Creed was forged on a fourth-century anvil in the heat of controversy. We will work through the details of its history in a future volume. Suffice it to say here merely that Arian understandings of the status of the Son of God arose in Alexandria (where an ascetic theologian named Arius promoted them), attracted theologians in the eastern Mediterranean, and, in the early 320s, piqued the interest of officials all over the Roman world. These understandings were censured by the bishops of two councils, the Council of Nicaea (325) and that of Constantinople (381), the latter of which declared its firm, trinitarian faith in what is now called the Nicene Creed. In response to the Arian view that Christ was *created* by and *lesser* than the Father, the drafters of this document declared (among other things), "We believe in . . . Jesus Christ, the only Son of God, eternally begotten of the Father, God from God, light from light, true God from true God,

22. Pelikan and Hotchkiss, 1:667–69.

begotten, not made, one in being with the Father." And "we believe in the Holy Spirit, the Lord, the giver of life, who proceeds from the Father" and thus is also fully God (a claim the Arians denied). The council fathers, that is, defined the faith against "Arianism."[23] Western leaders would add that the Spirit of God proceeds from the Father "and the Son" (*filioque*), changing the wording of the creed during the late sixth century, a move that gained prominence in much of Western Europe and was sanctioned by the popes of the early eleventh century (contributing to the church's Great Schism soon thereafter, in 1054, and dividing Eastern and Western Christianity ever since). Westerners have never used the Nicene Creed quite as often as the Apostles' Creed. Its fulsome definition of the doctrine of the Trinity, however, won the approval of the Orthodox churches (sans the *filioque* clause), which renders its confession the most universal symbol of the faith in all the world.

The Athanasian Creed is the longest of the so-called ecumenical creeds. Another trinitarian statement, it was once thought to be the work of Bishop Athanasius, archrival of the Arians, but is now thought to date to the fifth or sixth century. Its bulk makes it difficult to use in corporate worship. Its tone has repelled many cautious Christian readers. It was intended originally for use not as a creed but as a document that represented Athanasian faith. But its vigilant concern to guard the faith once delivered still functions as a symbol of the struggle over orthodoxy. "Whoever desires to be saved must above all things hold the catholic faith," it claims. "Unless one keeps it in its entirety inviolate," moreover, "one will assuredly perish eternally."[24] These creeds and many others—marked with varying degrees of precision and severity—have served the church for centuries as summaries and boundaries of the orthodox faith.

---

23. Pelikan and Hotchkiss, 1:670–72. As we will see in the next volume, by the early 380s there were several different versions of this heresy on offer. They differed so much from one another that specialists sometimes resist the use of blanket terms like "Arianism" to cover them all.

24. Pelikan and Hotchkiss, 1:673–77.

The impulse to regulate Christian faith and practice also led to the forming of the New Testament canon. The English word "canon" comes from the Greek word καvών, meaning "measuring rod" or "rule." And the New Testament canon is the list of books that measure up to standards implemented by the early church fathers: evident inspiration by the Spirit, most importantly—discerned by testing truthfulness, canonical consistency, and sanctifying power—and a certified apostolic pedigree. A basic consensus on the canon of the Hebrew Scriptures was achieved by about the second century (though a stable *arrangement* of its books took longer; the Eastern lists of Hebrew books have minor variations, and the canon of the Greek Old Testament was contested for centuries to come, and never quite resolved, except for Catholics at the Council of Trent in 1546), and the canon of the Greek Old Testament was contested for centuries to come, and never quite resolved, except for Catholics at the Council of Trent in 1546.[25] The New Testament canon came together much later, and largely in response to environmental pressure. Some of its material was believed to be inspired and authoritative for Christians shortly after it was written (see Col. 4:16; 1 Tim. 5:18; and 2 Pet. 3:16). Most of it was firm by the late second century. But the canon as a whole did not congeal in final form until the late fourth and early fifth centuries.[26]

25. The Greek Old Testament, also known as the Septuagint (the ancient Greek translation of the Old Testament writings), includes a number of items not found in Hebrew Scripture (some of which are not in all the oldest extant copies of the Greek Bible either—these copies vary quite a bit, and some include material that is not in any canon). Called deuterocanonical ("of the second canon," or canonical but secondary) and *anagignōskomena* ("readable, worthy to be read") by Catholics and Orthodox, apocryphal by Protestants ("obscure," or noncanonical), they were published in the Vulgate (the ancient Latin Bible of Jerome and his associates), despite Jerome's view that they should not be in the canon, and many subsequent editions of the Christian Bible as well. Most Protestant Reformers either excluded them completely or set them apart visibly from the main canon of Scripture, usually in between the testaments. On April 4, 1546, at the Council of Trent, Catholic leaders made a decree, *De Canonicis Scripturis* (Concerning the canonical Scriptures), in which they defined their Old Testament canon clearly and dogmatically (trans. at The Council of Trent, http://www.thecounciloftrent.com/ch4.htm).

26. On the complicated history of canon formation, start with Edmon L. Gallagher and John D. Meade, *The Biblical Canon Lists from Early Christianity: Texts and Analysis* (Oxford: Oxford University Press, 2017), which offers a detailed analysis of the early biblical canon lists themselves.

The first powerful incentive to decide upon an orthodox canon of Christian Scripture came from one who would later suffer censure as a heretic. Marcion of Sinope, a bishop's son on the Black Sea in the Greek region of Pontus, made a canon of his own as a guide to his philosophy (ca. 130–40). Convinced by a second-century Gnostic named Cerdo that the Old Testament god differed starkly from the God and father of Jesus in the Gospels—the former was cold, distant, militant, partial to the Jews, and concerned with physical needs, while the latter was full of love, accessible to all, and concerned with heavenly things—he organized a dualistic movement of the spirit, taught his followers to reject the Jewish god and his materialism, said that Jesus came to teach a way of life that freed the soul from its bondage to the flesh, and excluded from his canon any apostolic documents that contravened his message. Because Jesus only *appeared* to have been born of a virgin, encumbered with a body, and put to death in the flesh—things far too corporeal to warrant our assent—most of the Gospels must be scrapped. And inasmuch as other apostolic writings were too Jewish, too concerned with mundane life, they were cut from the Marcionite canon of Scripture as well. Paul of Tarsus, claimed Marcion, was called by the good god to clarify the true implications of Jesus' teaching. He was taken up to heaven on the road to Damascus, instructed by the savior, and sent back to earth to craft "The Gospel of the Lord" (the Gospel of Luke, some think, without its story of Christ's nativity and other fleshly elements) and ten holy letters (shortened versions of the ones then attributed to Paul minus 1 and 2 Timothy and Titus). These documents alone made the Marcionite canon, which incited church leaders to form a canon of their own.

Soon orthodox Christians placed Matthew, Mark, Luke, John, and most of Paul's epistles on a level of authority with Old Testament writings. Irenaeus and Tertullian attacked Marcion's views by comparing them to unrevised apostolic teaching.[27] And an anonymous, more

---

27. For example, Irenaeus, *Adversus haereses* 1.27; 3.2; Tertullian, *Adversus Marcionem*.

orthodox canon was composed (ca. 170, according to most). Called the Muratorian Canon, or the Muratorian Fragment, it includes all our New Testament books except Hebrews, James, and 1 and 2 Peter. It also includes the Apocalypse of Peter, however (a fragment of which survives, but is not in any Bible), and the Wisdom of Solomon (also called the Book of Wisdom, which is published in most editions of the Apocrypha).[28]

By the early fourth century, discussions about the canonization of New Testament books had become more sophisticated, though not yet unanimous. Eusebius of Caesarea, a bishop and historian, created a taxonomy in *History of the Church* (ca. 313) that reflects the state of learned conversation at the time. He distinguished what he called widely "recognized books" (*homologoumenoi*) from "disputed books" (*antilogoumenoi*) and those deemed specious or heretical. The recognized books were Matthew, Mark, Luke, John, Acts, the Pauline epistles, Hebrews, 1 Peter, 1 John, and John's Apocalypse (though Eusebius remarked that the status of the book of Revelation was contested). The disputed books were organized in two different groups: those widely yet not quite universally sanctioned—namely, James, 2 Peter, 2 and 3 John, and Jude—and others deemed spurious by most at the time: Acts of Paul, Shepherd of Hermas, Apocalypse of Peter, Epistle of Barnabas, Didache, and, by some, John's Apocalypse as well. The heretical list featured an array of bogus texts, such as the Gospels of Matthias, Thomas, and Peter.[29]

By the late fourth century, unanimity was near. Athanasius of Alexandria, the on-again, off-again, controversial bishop and opponent of the Arians, circulated an Easter letter in 367 in which he specified the very twenty-seven books later ruled the New Testament canon. "These are fountains of salvation," the bishop told his people, "that

28. The Muratorian Fragment is a seventh-century Latin translation of a late second-century Greek text, named for L. A. Muratori, who discovered it in Milan in the early eighteenth century. The translation of Bruce Metzger is found at Bible Research, http://www.bible-researcher.com /muratorian.html.

29. Eusebius of Caesarea, *Historia ecclesiastica* 3.25.

they who thirst may be satisfied with the living words they contain. In these alone is proclaimed the doctrine of godliness. Let no man add to these, neither let him take aught from these."[30] Several major church councils then adjudicated the canon, most importantly in Rome and Carthage in 382 and 397, respectively, sanctioning the twenty-seven books of Athanasius. The clergy in the East received the canon more slowly. They were less inclined than Westerners to dogmatize decrees of non-ecumenical councils. And the New Testament canons of the Orthodox in Syria, Armenia, Ethiopia, Egypt, and Georgia had minor variations. By the late fifth century, though, an overwhelming majority of believers, East and West, embraced the same New Testament. At the Quinisext Council held in Constantinople (692), moreover, Eastern bishops stamped the canon with approval.

In the providence of God and the power of the Spirit, the traditions by means of which the apostolic teaching shaped the faith, hope, and love of ancient followers of Jesus yielded a stable set of Scriptures by the time of the decline of the ancient Roman Empire (in the long fifth century—the city of Rome itself was sacked by Visigoths on August 24, 410). Most Christians now agreed that the canon was the main source of Christian faith and practice, the ultimate authority in ecclesial disputes, and the most reliable handbook of the teaching of the prophets and apostles of the Lord, not to mention Christ himself. This did not put an end to their diversity, however. They continued to debate the way the Spirit had presided over Scripture's canonization; the relative authority of extrabiblical customs in the teaching of the church; the place of popes, bishops, councils, and the faithful in discerning what the Spirit says in Scripture; and the best ways to transmit the elements of Scripture not codified in ancient Christian doctrine. Leaders longed for the Lord's help in navigating their differences, praying with the author of the Epistle to the Hebrews for a

---

30. Athanasius of Alexandria, Festal Letter 39; trans. at New Advent, http://www.newadvent.org/fathers/2806039.htm.

fuller, more mature Christian discipleship. "For though by this time you ought to be teachers," they would have reminded themselves, "you need someone to teach you again the basic elements of the oracles of God. You need milk, not solid food; for everyone who lives on milk, being still an infant, is unskilled in the word of righteousness. But solid food is for the mature, for those whose faculties have been trained by practice to distinguish good from evil. Therefore let us go on towards perfection," they exclaimed, "leaving behind the basic teaching about Christ, and not laying again the foundation: repentance from dead works and faith towards God, instruction about baptisms, laying on of hands, resurrection of the dead, and eternal judgement" (Heb. 5:12–6:2).

Interpreting the Word by the Spirit with the Church

The crumbling of the ancient Roman Empire meant chaos, especially for the faithful west of Constantinople. Arian and pagan tribes invaded from the north, wreaking havoc on the catholic civilization of Western Europe and Roman North Africa and worrying the faithful about the future of the church. If there ever was a time for agreement in the ranks—for a stable set of doctrines that would stem fear and confusion—it was now, and on the basis of a canonized Bible. The church was "one, holy, catholic, and apostolic," Christians claimed in an oft-repeated line from the Nicene Creed. Some of the church's Scripture was self-evident, nearly all of them affirmed. Some had yielded teaching codified by ecumenical councils. But some proved ambiguous—susceptible of more than one sound interpretation—and yet important to the practice of the faith nonetheless. Who retained the final say in presenting Scripture's mysteries? How much difference of opinion was permissible? What should Christians do, when their teachers disagreed, to determine what the Spirit was declaring in the Bible? The churches and their leaders had confronted similar questions since the time of the apostles. Heretics had long bent Scripture to their benefit. Catholics had responded that these heterodox exegetes "falsify the oracles of God, and prove themselves evil interpreters of the good word of revelation."[31] Theologians had offered up methods of exegesis. But now that the orthodox agreed on the kerygma, rules of faith, and canon of Scripture, expectations surged with respect to doctrinal unity. And now that their churches lacked protection from the Romans, the stakes of their quest for unanimity were raised. It is important not to exaggerate the discord and disintegration of the church as it entered what scholars used to call the "dark ages" of the post-Roman West. Christianity had always been much bigger than the West. Though the culture of the Romans did facilitate its rise—and its spread beyond the boundaries of their international empire—disciples took the gospel well beyond the Roman world from the beginning of their missionary movement. Furthermore, most now agreed about the teachings of their Savior, the doctrine of the Trinity, and the life of the world to come. And some of these beliefs were solidified further—for Christians East and West—at the ecumenical councils of the sixth to eighth centuries (all convened east of Rome, in Asia Minor, modern Turkey, now protected by the Eastern, or Byzantine, rulers). From far enough away, then, the church appeared strong, well prepared to meet the onslaughts of the post-Roman age.

Such strength was not enough, though, to guarantee unity, or even make it likely, in the centuries to come. In fact, the rest of catholic history could be told as a story of disciples with an old-fashioned, centripetal faith—and a passionate commitment to the *ideal* of unity—responding to centrifugal dynamics of success, accommodating changes in the church as it spread, spanned the globe, and adapted to new cultures and priorities. Most members of the body of Christ trusted in its unity. Their theologians taught them of its indefectibility. But many wanted freedom to inhabit that body—to nourish

31. Irenaeus, *Adversus haereses* 1.preface (see also 1.8.1); trans. at New Advent, http://www.newadvent.org/fathers/0103.htm.

it, clothe it, and present it to the world—in keeping with their own local customs and traditions. Just as Christians reached consensus on the New Testament canon, then, divisions in the way its finer points were interpreted undermined the oneness of the church in all but spirit. "I ask . . . that they may all be one," Christ himself had pleaded on the way to the cross. "As you, Father, are in me and I am in you, may they also be in us, so that the world may believe that you have sent me" (John 17:20–21). Most honored this prayer and believed in its fulfillment. They trusted that the Spirit would take them into all the truth on the basis of the Word, thus unifying the body of Christ all around the world. But they often disagreed about what the Spirit said.

The first major episode of postcanonical conflict transpired over the course of the fifth and sixth centuries and centered on Augustine's view of predestination. A British theologian named Pelagius moved to Rome in about 380 and soon became concerned about its people's moral laxity. He engaged in strict asceticism and gained a minor following. When Rome was sacked in 410, he fled with a follower named Caelestius to Carthage and sparked a major controversy that spread across the Roman world by teaching an extreme form of moral rigorism. He said that everyone can live a sinless life and find salvation without waiting for a special interposition of God's grace (though he granted that the freedom of the will, moral law, and Christian nurture and instruction were results of God's grace that helped Christians on their way). Augustine and his followers resisted this teaching. They said that even in the garden of Eden—before the first sin and tragic fall of the race—Adam and Eve needed supernatural grace to live for God. East of Eden, furthermore, human need had grown worse. On account of original sin, we are now born depraved. We have disordered affections, minds and wills inclined to sin. We never choose to honor God unless our hearts are transformed. God foresaw this predicament before he made the world. In his mercy, though, he chose to create us anyway and then rescue a portion of the race by his grace. There is nothing we can do to earn this blessing retroactively. The elect owe their status to the sovereignty of God, and their righteousness to God's decree to transform their souls and help them want to live according to his plan for their lives.

In the near term, Augustine's view prevailed in the Western church. Pelagius and his men were condemned at major councils held in Carthage (418) and Ephesus (431). But the doctrine they espoused never simply disappeared. Nor did the biblical exegesis that supported it. A group of monks in southern Gaul (near the city of Marseilles), in fact, championed a compromise that proved quite resilient. Concerned about the moral implications of Augustine's view of predestination, they reemphasized the freedom sinners have to repent and make good upon the grace God has woven into the world without waiting for an extra, supernatural act of God. Saving grace was required, of course, the "Gallicanis" granted, but seekers could elicit it by turning to the Lord. John Cassian and Vincent of Lérins were their spokesmen, the latter of whom coined a test of orthodoxy (in controversies with Arians and others) that he thought would make their compromise position more tenable. Called the "Vincentian Canon" (ca. 434), it stipulated that "care must especially be had that that be held which was believed everywhere [*ubique*], always [*semper*], and by all [*ab omnibus*]" faithful Christians.[32] Augustine's view of sin and election failed this test, and so should not be required of the faithful moving forward. Augustinians like Prosper of Aquitaine resisted this Gallicani compromise (also called "Massilian" for its locus in Marseilles), contending that it downplayed the consequences of sin and gratuity of grace. Both groups appealed to the canon, rule of

---

32. Vincent of Lérins, *Comonitoria* 2; trans. at New Advent, http://www.newadvent.org/fathers /3506.htm. Several scholars have reminded us that Vincent stood closer to Augustine than to Pelagius on the issues under discussion. His so-called semi-pelagianism, a later attribution based on misinformation, was invented by opponents. See Thomas G. Guarino, *Vincent of Lérins and the Development of Christian Doctrine*, Foundations of Theological Exegesis and Christian Spirituality (Grand Rapids: Baker Academic, 2013), xvii–xviii, xxi, xxvii.

faith, and traditions of the church. But they disagreed about how to handle these authorities and settle their dispute. Prosper concluded that the popes were the ultimate interpreters of Scripture. The Gallicanis countered that consensus should be sought. But their Vincentian Canon proved difficult to use, and the Gallicani doctrine was condemned at the Council of Orange (529).[33] This controversy plagued the church for centuries to come. During the late Middle Ages it resurfaced yet again, and promoters of the Gallicani doctrine were condemned—and labeled "semi-pelagian"—by Protestant and Roman Catholic leaders.

The next major episode of postcanonical controversy centered on the veneration of icons by Christians. As Islamic forces overspread the Byzantine world, Eastern rulers sought to purify their churches of corruption (which they blamed for Christian losses) and avoid adding fuel to the conflict with their foes (who were largely aniconic, or opposed to using icons). Iconoclastic sentiment intensified in fits and starts, especially among those most worried about Islam, yielding a ban on Christian icons in the late 720s by the Byzantine emperor Leo III. Such images themselves, of course, are not found in Scripture, and opponents of their use (often called "iconoclasts," which means "image destroyers") claimed that paying them respect was like bowing down to idols. Still, God had made humans in his "image" and "likeness" (Gen. 1:26–27). Moses put images of angels in the tabernacle (Exod. 25–31, 35–40). And Christ himself is said to be the "icon" (εἰκών) of God (Col. 1:15). Few artists made icons of the person of the Father, who does not have a body and "dwells in unapproachable light, whom no one has ever seen or can see," wrote Paul (1 Tim. 6:16). Depictions of the Father were forbidden much later (at the Eastern Synod of Moscow, in 1667). But many came to believe that the incarnation of God in the person of Jesus Christ made a way for depictions of the Savior and his saints. They also said that

33. Denzinger, *Sources of Catholic Dogma*, §§173b–200 (pp. 75–81).

the handling of the relevant Scripture texts should be governed—in the main—by tradition.

By the mid-sixth century, tradition had begun to assume a life of its own not far beneath the canon and the bishops as a norm in the development of doctrine. A number of different sources could be cited in this regard, not least the canon of Vincent first deployed by Massilians. The bishops at the Second Council of Constantinople (553) claimed, when promulgating doctrine, to "hold and declare the faith given from the beginning by the great God and our Savior Jesus Christ to the Holy Apostles, and preached by them in the whole world; which the sacred Fathers both confessed and explained, and handed down to the holy churches."[34] And many later theologians, when working on matters not discussed in the canon, resorted to tradition in support of their opinions.

John of Damascus, for example, the most important of the eighth-century champions of icons, appealed to tradition in his battle with opponents. In his *On Holy Images* (ca. 730), he aggregated statements from the fathers on their use. And in *The Orthodox Faith* (ca. 740s), he explained that while conservatives wanted "nothing beyond" the teachings of the "Law and Prophets and Apostles and Evangelists," they refused to flout what John called the "everlasting boundaries" of proper interpretation or haughtily "[overpass] the divine tradition (Prov. 22:28)."[35] By the late eighth century, John's instincts won the day as the leaders of Nicaea II (787) exalted the tradition in support of sacred icons. Referring to the fathers of the church as "inspired," and contending that the Spirit "dwells in" the tradition, they condemned those "who dare to think or teach otherwise," underwriting the veneration of icons by Christians.[36] Even so, opposition to icons never fell away. Emperor Leo V led another purge of icons in the early

---

34. Denzinger, *Sources of Catholic Dogma*, §212 (p. 85).

35. John of Damascus, "The Orthodox Faith" (part of Πηγή Γνώσεως; see above) 1.1; trans. at New Advent, http://www.newadvent.org/fathers/33041.htm.

36. Denzinger, *Sources of Catholic Dogma*, §§302–4 (pp. 121–22).

ninth century (814–42). In the sixteenth century, many Protestants destroyed priceless icons, crucifixes, statuary, and paintings in the name of abolishing idolatry.

A third major episode of postcanonical dissidence pertained to the use of the *filioque* clause. I have dealt with this above and will treat it in detail in the future volume of this project. I mention it again here to make the observation that this epochal, church-dividing, theological conflict (which led to the Great Schism of 1054) took its rise not mainly from an exegetical row (though the Bible was involved) but from debate about the authority of Western church leaders to change the liturgy, the creed, and thus the doctrine of the Trinity without seeking input from the churches of the East. Not only had tradition taken on a life of its own, then, by this time in history. Traditions East and West had now diversified dramatically, and many doctrinal feuds involved discussion about the canon, the authority of bishops and traditions in its use, *and* the relative authority of contrary bishops and traditions in the teaching of the church. The development of doctrine proved as complex as ever.

No one symbolized this complication better than Peter Abelard, whose *Sic et non* (Yes and no; ca. 1120) undermined the faith of many in the unified witness of the teachers of the church. Posing 158 theological questions, he arrayed the church fathers on opposing sides of each of them, demonstrating clearly that they contradicted themselves and encouraging a dialectical search for the truth. Despite the errors many frequently decried in *Sic et non*, it awakened earnest students to the problems that attend glib appeals to "the tradition," or "the witness of the fathers," and was placed much later on the Index of Forbidden Books (*Index librorum prohibitorum*).[37] In the meantime, it fueled the rise of orthodox, organized compilations of "sentences" on Scripture and tradition culled from early church fathers, learned

---

37. Peter Abelard, *Sic et non* (ca. 1120); partial trans. in "Peter Abelard (1079–1142): Prologue to Sic et Non," at Medieval Sourcebook, https://sourcebooks.fordham.edu/source/Abelard-SicetNon-Prologue.asp.

commentaries upon the most famous of these sentences, and summaries of doctrine by theologians eager to show that Christian faith
coheres. The most influential of these was the *Four Books of Sentences*
by Bishop Peter Lombard (ca. 1155–57), an Italian serving in Paris,
which became the leading dogmatic textbook in Europe and inspired
scores of commentaries in centuries to come.[38]

Many now yearned for a stable and reliable way to inculcate the
Word by the Spirit in the church. There are always some who face
ambiguity with ease, keeping faith with God and neighbor in the
midst of uncertainty, conflict, and mystery. But most want guidance. And by the thirteenth century, many Westerners attained it
in a resolution regarding the relationship between holy Scripture,
tradition, and the church near to that of the Italian Thomas Aquinas, for whom orthodox tradition, determined by the church, was
a source of authority analogous to Scripture. It was varied, to be
sure, and shaped doctrine indirectly through the dictates of popes,
church councils, and other organs of the Catholic magisterium
(which by now stood apart from the bishops of the East, who favored a somewhat more conciliar, less papal, understanding of the
promulgation of doctrine). In the main, it was used to guide biblical
exegesis. But it guided nonetheless, as it harmonized conflicts under
the aegis of the Church in favor of Roman Catholic orthodoxy. As
Thomas wrote famously in *Summa Theologiae* (1265–74), "Doctrine
is especially based upon arguments from authority, inasmuch as its
principles are obtained by revelation: thus we ought to believe on
the authority of those [teachers] to whom the revelation has been
made."[39] He insisted that such conduits of special revelation "ought
not to say about God anything which is not found in Holy Scripture

---

38. Peter Lombard, *Libri quattuor sententiarum* (ca. 1155–57); partial trans. available for purchase at Franciscan Archive, https://www.franciscan-archive.org/lombardus/I-Sent.html; full
trans.: Peter Lombard, *The Sentences*, trans. Giulio Silano, 4 vols. (Toronto: Pontifical Institute
of Mediaeval Studies, 2007–10).

39. Thomas Aquinas, *Summa Theologiae* I, q. 1, a. 8; trans. at New Advent, http://www.newadvent
.org/summa/1001.htm#article8.

either explicitly or implicitly."[40] But he claimed that the bishops usually followed this rule. "In every council of the Church," he said, "a symbol of faith has been drawn up to meet some prevalent error condemned in the council at that time. Hence subsequent councils are not to be described as making a new symbol of faith; but what was implicitly contained in the first symbol was explained by some addition directed against rising heresies."[41] Church teaching explicated the deposit of the faith. And even unwritten tradition played a part in this affair, though always under the tutelage of apostolic heirs. "The Apostles, led by the inward instinct of the Holy Ghost, handed down to the churches certain instructions which they did not put in writing, but which have been ordained, in accordance with the observance of the Church as practiced by the faithful as time went on."[42] Thus tradition always functioned as a necessary, apostolic guide to revelation when deployed by those entrusted with the teaching of the church. God's Spirit gave the Word through the bishops of the Catholic Church, who inculcated Scripture in accordance with tradition.

By the late Middle Ages, even critics of the papacy and prophets of conciliarism (rule by church councils) rooted their positions in the soil of tradition. Academics disagreed about the relative authority of popes, church councils, Christian princes, canon law, and the doctors of the church in discerning church tradition. Some questioned whether anything not based on the Bible was essential to salvation. During the Western papal schism (1378–1417) many sought a more episcopal approach to solving internal doctrinal disputes. Still, most parties involved laid claim to the past. Even those at the Council of Constance (1414–18), convened at the apex of conciliar dominion

40. Aquinas, *Summa Theologiae* I, q. 36, a. 2; trans. at New Advent, http://www.newadvent.org/summa/1036.htm#article2.

41. Aquinas, *Summa Theologiae* I, q. 36, a. 2; trans. at New Advent, http://www.newadvent.org/summa/1036.htm#article2.

42. Aquinas, *Summa Theologiae* III, q. 25, a. 3; trans. at New Advent, http://www.newadvent.org/summa/4025.htm.

to put an end, once and for all, to the Western papal schism, re-sorted to "the catholic faith," councils, and the fathers—condemning the English theologian John Wycliffe and the Czech, or Bohemian, theologian Jan Hus, who resisted their rendition of late medieval catholicity—compelling future pontiffs to profess their allegiance to orthodox tradition. "As long as I am in this fragile life," they had to pledge, "I will firmly believe and hold the catholic faith, according to the traditions of the apostles, of the general councils and of other holy fathers, especially of the eight holy universal councils . . . as well as of the general councils at the Lateran, Lyons and Vienne." Furthermore, "I will preserve this faith unchanged to the last dot and will confirm, defend and preach it to the point of death and the shedding of my blood."[43]

Thus when Martin Luther claimed not only that the papacy had erred but that councils, canon law, and the mass itself were flawed, pandemonium ensued, tearing scabs from several wounds on the global body of Christ that had formed very slowly and had never quite healed. Luther's brief against the Catholic Church was leveled most loudly in the Ninety-Five Theses (1517). Upset about the sale of indulgences in Germany to raise funds for Rome, he contended that this practice misconstrued Christian teaching on salvation by grace. But his case against the Church's view of Scripture and tradition would continue to develop over the next several years. At the Leipzig Disputation versus Johann Eck of Ingolstadt (1519), he opposed the supremacy of popes and church councils. Then he published three treatises in 1520 against the tyranny of Rome over German-speaking Christians, the "Babylonian"/Roman captivity of the church, and the freedom of the Christian to live for God without subservience to man-made rules. Before these tracts were released, Pope Leo X

---

43. Decreed in session 39, October 9, 1417. The Latin original with translation is provided in *Decrees of the Ecumenical Councils*, ed. Norman P. Tanner, 2 vols. (London: Sheed & Ward, 1990), 1:442. The eighth of the "holy universal councils" mentioned in this statement is Constantinople IV (879–80), not recognized as a universal council in the East.

condemned him in a papal bull (*Exsurge Domine*, 1520), which summarized his "heresy" in forty-one doctrines and threatened to exclude him from the sacraments if he did not recant in sixty days. Luther burned the bull publicly six months later. He was excommunicated early in 1521 and commanded to appear before the emperor at Worms. In response to the pope's condemnation of his views, he claimed to "preach nothing new" but asserted that the Bible had been muffled by the curia—even by the pope—and that Scripture alone, not the Roman magisterium, was infallible and determinative in matters of faith and practice. "This is my answer to those also who accuse me of rejecting all the holy teachers of the church," Luther wrote. "I do not reject them. But everyone, indeed, knows that at times they have erred, as men will; therefore, I am ready to trust them only when they give me evidence for their opinions from Scripture, which has never erred. . . . Scripture alone is the true lord and master of all writings and doctrine on earth."[44] Before Emperor Charles V, he added, "Unless I am convinced by the testimony of the Scriptures or by clear reason (for I do not trust either in the pope or in councils alone, since it is well known that they have often erred and contradicted themselves), I am bound by the Scriptures I have quoted and my conscience is captive to the Word of God."[45] This is standard fare today among the heirs of Luther's doctrine. But in 1521, it made him an outlaw.

Church officials at the Council of Trent (1545–63) soon circled the wagons, protecting an inviolate, concatenated concept of catholic tradition. "Following the example of the orthodox fathers," they decreed in an effort to repel Luther's teaching, "the council accepts

44. From the introduction to Martin Luther, *Grund und Ursache aller Artikel D. Martin Luthers so durch romische Bulle unrechtlich verdammt sind*, Luther's German translation of his *Assertio Omnium Articulorum M. Lutheri, per Bullam Leonis X, Novissimam Damnatorum*, in *D. Martin Luthers Werke: Kritische Gesamtausgabe*, 69 vols. (bound as 88) (Weimar: Hermann Böhlaus Nachfolger, 1883–2009; hereafter *WA*), 7:94–115; trans. in Martin Luther, *Career of the Reformer II*, in *Luther's Works* (hereafter *LW*), ed. George W. Forell (Philadelphia: Fortress, 1958), 32:3–98 (quotation from pp. 11–12).

45. *WA*, 7:838; trans. in *LW*, 32:112.

and venerates with a like feeling of piety and reverence" both the contents of the Vulgate (the common Latin Bible, Apocrypha included) and "traditions" of "faith and conduct, as either directly spoken by Christ or dictated by the holy Spirit, which have been preserved in unbroken sequence" in the church. And "if anyone should not accept" the Vulgate and "aforesaid traditions" of the church, "let him be anathema." Protestants were severed from the Roman Catholic Church. "No one, relying on his personal judgment," the council fathers continued, "shall dare to interpret the sacred scriptures either by twisting its text to his individual meaning in opposition to that which has been and is held by holy mother church, whose function is to pass judgment on the true meaning and interpretation of the sacred scriptures; or by giving it meanings contrary to the unanimous consent of the fathers. . . . Whoever acts contrary to this decision is to be publicly named by religious superiors and punished by the penalties prescribed by law."[46] More than three centuries later, these strictures were confirmed at the First Vatican Council (1869–70). "Supernatural revelation," its delegates explained, "according to the belief of the universal church, as declared by the sacred council of Trent, is contained in written books and unwritten traditions." And "that meaning of holy scripture must be held to be the true one, which holy mother church held and holds."[47]

Luther had not intended to disown the tradition. On the contrary, he thought his evangelical reformers held the best claim to rightful continuity with the past. But as they made use of what they came to call the Scripture principle, wielding God's Word to weed and prune the tradition and revise Christian doctrine with their own exegesis, they accelerated the doctrinal diversity of Christendom—and expanded the means by which the Spirit was discerned—at a rate

46. Council of Trent, session 4, April 8, 1546, in Tanner, *Decrees of the Ecumenical Councils*, 2:663–64.

47. First Vatican Council, session 3, April 24, 1870, in Tanner, *Decrees of the Ecumenical Councils*, 2:806.

unprecedented in history. The Reformer Jean Calvin, in an address to the French king Francis I prefixed to his *Institutes* (1536),[48] did "not at all doubt" that his Reformation doctrine sounded new to Catholic critics, "since to them both Christ himself and his gospel are new." But it clearly had the weight of Christian history on its side. "All the fathers," he insisted in a hyperbolic flourish, "with one heart have abhorred and with one voice have detested the fact that God's Holy Word has been contaminated by the subtleties of sophists and involved in the squabbles of dialecticians. When they attempt nothing in life but to enshroud and obscure the simplicity of Scripture with endless contentions and worse than sophistic brawls, do they keep themselves within these borders?" Calvin queried. "If the fathers were now brought back to life," he concluded, they would surely sympathize with the Reformers.[49] Still, even high-church Protestants subscribed to tradition only insofar as the latter followed Scripture. As Richard Hooker clarified in his Elizabethan *Laws of Ecclesiastical Polity* (1593 ff.), "Least therefore the name of tradition should be offensive . . . consideringe how farre by some it . . . is abused, wee meane by traditions ordinances made in the prime of Christian religion, established with that authoritie which Christ hath left his Church for matters indifferent, and in that consideration requisite to be observed till like authoritie see just and reasonable cause to alter them." Traditions were derived from the teaching of the apostles and revisable based upon the very same thing—though, for Anglicans like Hooker, only in rightly ordered ways by ecclesial officials.[50]

Even the most radical Protestants interpreted the Bible with assistance from the past. But the Reformation raised some rather

48. The address to King Francis was included in subsequent editions as well.

49. From the *Praefatio ad Christianissimum Regem Franciae, qua hic ei liber pro confessione fidei offertur*, in Calvin's *Christianae Religionis Institutio* (Basel: [T. Platteru & B. Lasium], 1536), 5–41; trans. in John Calvin, *Institutes of the Christian Religion*, 2 vols., ed. John T. McNeill, trans. Ford Lewis Battles, Library of Christian Classics (Philadelphia: Westminster, 1960), 1:9–31 (quotation from 16, 22).

50. Richard Hooker, *Of the Lawes of Ecclesiastical Polity*, preface and books 1–5, 2 vols., ed. Georges Edelen and W. Speed Hill, Folger Library Edition of the Works of Richard Hooker (Cambridge, MA: Belknap Press of Harvard University Press, 1977), 2:302.

disconcerting questions. Did the church's rightful teachers ever get the Bible wrong? Did popes and councils err? And if they did, what should be done?

Listening to the Spirit in an Era of Improvement

As Protestantism spread, so did the spirit of reform, critical thinking, and revision of the church's teaching ministry that stemmed from the crises of the late "Middle Ages" (a term that had been coined amid these European culture wars by those who appealed to ancient sources of renewal, leaping over a millennium of meantime to do so). And in the age of "the Enlightenment," this spirit ran away from its ecclesiastical home, as historicism and evolutionary ways of thinking undermined the faith of many in traditionary knowledge, whether in Scripture or the dogmatic history of the church. Western Europe's literati dared to think for themselves, as Immanuel Kant suggested.[51] They distrusted the traditions of medieval Christendom, employed critical methods in the study of the Bible, and labored to advance upon the thinking of the past. Many thought that human knowledge and behavior were improving. And they hoped that human reason and scientific learning would enable them to overcome the worst of world history. The best known among them were freethinking intellectuals in the seventeenth, eighteenth, and early nineteenth centuries: Spinoza, Voltaire, Locke, Hume, Kant, and Hegel. But many church leaders, too, became developmental thinkers, handing on the faith in more historical, progressive, less authoritarian styles—and promoting new methods of listening to the Spirit.

In the grand scheme of things, only a fraction of the people of God participated in this Western intellectual movement—at least in the beginning. Many Christians lived beyond the reach of European

51. Immanuel Kant, "Beantwortung der Frage: Was ist Aufklärung?," Berlinische Monatsschrift 12 (1784): 481–94; for trans., see What Is Enlightenment, available from Columbia University, http://www.columbia.edu/acis/ets/CCREAD/etscc/kant.html.

culture. And few, even in Europe, read the work of the elite. Most of the Orthodox, for instance, carried on much as before. They continued to affirm the importance of perpetuating orthodox tradition. And they championed the role of ancient practices in doing so, especially ascetic and devotional exercises. "Tradition," wrote Metropolitan Philaret of Moscow, "does not consist uniquely in visible and verbal transmissions of the teachings, the rules, institutions and rites: it is at the same time an invisible and actual communication of grace and sanctification."[52] These priorities were detailed in the *Philokalia* (1782), an Orthodox compendium of texts by spiritual masters of the hesychast tradition of prayer without ceasing as a means to union with God (such as Gregory Palamas, who defended hesychasm in the fourteenth century against the likes of Barlaam of Seminara). Compiled by the fathers of Mount Athos in Greece (mainly Nicodemus the Hagiorite and Macarius of Corinth), the *Philokalia* facilitated an ancient manner of Christian prayer and piety—lost to the philosophes of early modern Europe—made famous in an anonymous Russian novel, *The Way of a Pilgrim* (1884).[53]

But "modern" ways of thinking did filter through the church—slowly but surely, drip by drip—in the West and its colonies. And mainstream Christians began to reconceive tradition not so much as a deposit that is meant to be preserved as an ongoing process of clarifying and explicating apostolic teaching (with assistance from believers outside the church hierarchy). John Henry Newman, a convert to and cardinal in the Roman Catholic Church, is the best-known symbol of this modern transformation. In his *Essay on the Development of Christian Doctrine* (1845), he suggested that the teaching of the Church has improved over time and that her doctrine grows

52. Quoted in English in Georges Florovsky, *Puti Russkago Bogoslovia* (Paris: YMCA Press, 1937), 178.

53. For English versions of these sources, see Saint Nikodimos of the Holy Mountain and Saint Makarios of Corinth, comps., *The Philokalia*, trans. G. E. H. Palmer, Philip Sherrard, Kallistos Ware, et al., 3 vols. (London: Faber and Faber, 1979–84); Olga Savin, trans., *"The Way of a Pilgrim" and "The Pilgrim Continues His Way"* (Boston: Shambhala, 2001).

clearer and more detailed with age. "Time is necessary," he wrote, "for the full comprehension and perfection of great ideas." Especially with respect to church teaching, he emphasized, "the highest and most wonderful truths, though communicated to the world once for all by inspired teachers, could not be comprehended all at once by the recipients, but, as being received and transmitted by minds not inspired and through media which were human, have required only the longer time and deeper thought for their full elucidation." He drove this point home with a now-famous metaphor. "It is indeed sometimes said that the stream is clearest near the spring," he admitted. Nonetheless,

> this image . . . does not apply to the history of a philosophy or belief, which on the contrary is more equable, and purer, and stronger, when its bed has become deep, and broad, and full. It necessarily rises out of an existing state of things, and for a time savours of the soil. Its vital element needs disengaging from what is foreign and temporary. . . . Its beginnings are no measure of its capabilities, nor of its scope. . . . From time to time it makes essays which fail, and are in consequence abandoned. . . . In time it enters upon strange territory; points of controversy alter their bearing; parties rise and fall around it; dangers and hopes appear in new relations; and old principles reappear under new forms. It changes with them in order to remain the same. In a higher world it is otherwise, but here below to live is to change, and to be perfect is to have changed often.[54]

Newman was not a relativist, leveler, or liberal. He submitted to the papacy and served as a cardinal. He studied church history, though, specializing in fourth-century trinitarian doctrine, and he knew that in the past the heat of controversy had often helped to purify and clarify the teaching of the church. He also knew the magisterium had

54. John Henry Newman, *An Essay on the Development of Christian Doctrine*, 6th ed., Notre Dame Series in the Great Books (Notre Dame, IN: University of Notre Dame Press, 1989), 29–30, 40.

made some big mistakes and that, in seasons of confusion, the religion of the faithful kept the church on course. In "On Consulting the Faithful in Matters of Doctrine" (1859), he contended that the piety of Christians "is one of the witnesses to the fact of the tradition of revealed doctrine." Their "consensus," furthermore, when the going gets tough, "is the voice of the Infallible Church." The teaching office "is more happy," he appended in a hint to the bishops, "when she has such enthusiastic partisans about her . . . than when she cuts off the faithful from the study of her divine doctrines and the sympathy of her divine contemplations, and requires from them a *fides implicita* [implicit faith] in her word, which in the educated classes will terminate in indifference, and in the poorer in superstition."[55]

Conservatives in Rome viewed Newman with suspicion. For as Jacques Bossuet, Bishop of Meaux, had put it for them, most notably in *History of the Variations of the Protestant Churches* (1688), Catholic teaching is "always the same" (*semper eadem*), which made it far more credible, reliable, and sure than the multiple alternatives on offer from the Protestants.[56] Developmental thinking, furthermore, had paved a way for not just doctrinal diversity but modernism and liberalism. And some Catholic thinkers later radicalized a Newmanesque notion of tradition, undercutting age-old doctrines in the process. The French priest Alfred Loisy and the Irish Catholic convert and Jesuit Father George Tyrrell, both well-known academics, were removed from the Church for developmental views. The French philosopher Maurice Blondel, a married layman, would receive the last rites. But his *History and Dogma* (1904) criticized both "historicists" and old-fashioned "extrinsicists" (apologists for static, inorganic church tradition) in

55. John Henry Newman, "On Consulting the Faithful in Matters of Doctrine," *Rambler*, 3rd ser., 1 (July 1859): 198–230, quoted here from its definitive, critical edition, John Henry Newman, *On Consulting the Faithful in Matters of Doctrine*, ed. John Coulson (Kansas City: Sheed and Ward, 1961), 63, 106. This principle (of the importance of the consensus of the faithful) is one with which the Orthodox agree.

56. Jacques Bénigne Bossuet, *Histoire des variations des églises protestantes*, 2 vols. (Paris: Chez la veuve de Sebastien Mabre-Cramoisy, 1688).

favor of a theory of tradition as "vital reality," a living organism that evolves over time under the guidance of the Spirit and whose truth is verified in Christian practice, or action.[57] Many say that the antimodern statements of Pope Pius X, such as *Lamentabili Sane* (1907) and *Pascendi Dominici Gregis* (1907), assailed Blondel. For, perhaps most importantly, officials at Vatican I (1869–70) had banned progressive views of doctrine in no uncertain terms. "That meaning of the sacred dogmas is ever to be maintained," they insisted quite clearly, "which has once been declared by holy mother church, and there must never be any abandonment of this sense under the pretext or in the name of a more profound understanding." Further, "if anyone says that it is possible that at some time, given the advancement of knowledge, a sense may be assigned to the dogmas propounded by the church which is different from that which the church has understood and understands: let him be anathema."[58]

Not just left-leaning Catholics but even the most conservative Protestants were subject to this ruling. For the latter placed Scripture over creeds, confessions, and other forms of tradition, historicizing them all and thus continuing to transform their churches' teaching ministries. The ones in universities advocated the value of independent, critical thinking, improving on the past by means of humanistic scholarship. Those in congregations or in new, modern seminaries perpetuated their churches' *own* confessional traditions. But they often criticized other churches as they did so—a practice then common in every major branch of Christendom—attempting to revise the larger catholic tradition. Philip Schaff, for example, perhaps the best-known Protestant at work in the churches to address these issues during the nineteenth century, valorized tradition more than many of his peers. He believed that it was pulsing well past the Church of Rome, though,

57. Maurice Blondel, *Histoire et Dogme* (1904), as presented in *"The Letter on Apologetics" and "History and Dogma,"* trans. Alexander Dru and Illtyd Trethowan (New York: Holt, Rinehart and Winston, 1964), 267, 275.

58. First Vatican Council, session 3, April 24, 1870, in Tanner, *Decrees of the Ecumenical Councils*, 2:809, 811.

ascending to a higher, "evangelical-catholic" future. After moving from Berlin to accept a teaching post at a German Reformed seminary in central Pennsylvania, he released a short treatise titled *What Is Church History? A Vindication of the Idea of Historical Development* (1846), appearing at the start like his Catholic colleague Newman. "So precisely as the single Christian does not become complete at a stroke," he contended, "but only by degrees, the church, as the complex of all Christians, must admit and require too a gradual development." This process "is *organic*," Schaff echoed Newman further. "Christianity is a new creation, that unfolds itself continually more and more from within." Not content with a Rome-bound theory of tradition, though, Schaff claimed "the main stream" of *his* catholic river, although "formed first by the Greek-Roman universal church," had wended through "Romano-Germanic Catholicism" only to flow more recently in "evangelical Protestantism."[59]

A passionate ecumenist, Schaff proved friendlier to those in other churches than the bulk of his contemporaries. Most nineteenth-century Protestants were stoutly anti-Catholic, using Scripture and tradition not simply to surpass but to tear down much of the history of the Roman Catholic Church. Charles Porterfield Krauth is a well-known example. Like Newman, Schaff, and others, he adopted a developmental view of Christian doctrine. In his massive work on *The Conservative Reformation and Its Theology* (1871), he explained that "the identity of the Church faith resembles not the sameness of a rock, but rather the living identity of a man. The babe and the adult are identical," he underlined to stress continuity in Protestant theology.

They are the same being in different stages of maturity: that which constitutes the individual does not change. . . . Adult perfection is

---

59. Philip Schaff, *What Is Church History? A Vindication of the Idea of Historical Development*, trans. John W. Nevin (Philadelphia: J. B. Lippincott and Co., 1846), 87, 91, 106–7. An expansion of a German lecture given in Mercersburg, this treatise was released first in English.

reached not by amputations and ingraftings, but by growth, in which the identifying energy conforms everything to its own nature. The faith of the Church now is identical with what it was in the Apostolic time, but the relation of identity does not preclude growth—it only excludes change of identity. . . . In a word, the advances are wrought, not by change in the Church faith, but by the perpetual activity of that faith, a faith which because it is incapable of change itself, assimilates more and more to it the consciousness of the Church, her system of doctrine, her language, and her life.[60]

Doctrine grows without change, a paradox resembling the argument of Newman. Krauth clarified, however, that as the faith grew it also outgrew the many errors of the Roman Catholic Church, escaping from the "Babylon" of late-medieval blight. During the Protestant Reformation, "the fire of the Divine Word destroyed the accumulated rubbish of tradition, swept away the hay, wood, and stubble, which the hand of man had gathered on the foundation and heaped over the temple, and the gold, silver, and precious stones of the true house of God appeared."[61] This sounds harsh today. But it was commonplace among most early modern Protestants. And as nineteenth-century Catholic leaders "grew" their Mariology (codifying the doctrine of the immaculate conception in 1854) and strengthened their commitment to the popes' jurisdiction (codifying the doctrine of papal infallibility in 1870), this anti-Catholic tendency increased.

The most important Protestant thinker to write about these issues for twentieth-century readers was the Swiss Reformed churchman and professor Karl Barth. In his *Church Dogmatics* (1932–67), Barth took on board a progressive view of doctrine. But in struggling against the modern Protestant domestication of God and his Word (by liberal predecessors who would only speak of God "from below," on the basis

60. Charles P. Krauth, *The Conservative Reformation and Its Theology: As Represented in the Augsburg Confession, and in the History and Literature of the Evangelical Lutheran Church* (Philadelphia: J. B. Lippincott, 1871), 270.

61. Krauth, *Conservative Reformation and Its Theology*, 14, 19.

of experience and consciousness), he insisted on the power and priority of Scripture over all other rivals—including church tradition. "The present-day witnesses of the Word of God can and should look back to the witnesses of the same Word who preceded them," he granted right away. "These fathers and brethren have a definite authority, the authority of prior witnesses . . . who have to be respected." But the weight of their tradition and the authority of the church must never be confused with the authority of Scripture. The Word of God "is given to the Church in such a way that it is always His Word as against its word." Underneath the Word of God the church does have authority. She "exercises it," though, in obedience to the Word, "by claiming for [her]self not a direct, but only a mediate authority, not a material but a formal, not an absolute but a relative." Hence "what we know as dogma is in principle fallible and is therefore neither final nor unalterable," he claimed. "Every Church confession can be regarded only as a stage on a road which as such can be relativised and succeeded by a further stage in the form of an altered confession."[62] This argument was not just academic for Barth. In the face of German Christians who accommodated the faith to the Nazi regime, he had helped in the drafting of the Barmen Declaration (1934), a new church confession that improved Christian witness to the Lordship of Christ over all earthly powers.[63]

Before the mid-twentieth century, Roman Catholics had a rough time gaining much ground with Newman's understanding of doctrine, getting past the strictures set at Trent and Vatican I, and incorporating the findings of modern scholarship on Scripture in the teaching of the church. The weight of tradition had many spinning their wheels or,

62. Karl Barth, *Die Kirchliche Dogmatik*, I/2 (Zürich: Evangelischer Verlag A. G. Zollikon, 1938), §20; trans., *Church Dogmatics*, vol. I/2, ed. G. W. Bromiley and T. F. Torrance, trans. G. T. Thomson and Harold Knight (New York: Charles Scribner's Sons, 1956), 538–660 (quotations from 573, 579, 586, 593, 657–59).

63. *Theologische Erklärung zur gegenwärtigen Lage der Deutschen Evangelischen Kirche (Barmer Theologische Erklärung)*; trans. at Internet Sacred Text Archive, http://www.sacred-texts.com/chr/barmen.htm.

depending on one's point of view, standing fast on principle amid the winds of change. In the spirit of renewal, though, or *ressourcement*—an effort to improve Catholic teaching by recovering older sources of exegesis and spiritual theology—a few Catholic thinkers sought to update the Church's way of catechizing the faithful, curtailing its reliance on polemical materials. Hans Urs von Balthasar and Henri de Lubac were the best known among them. Karl Rahner, Yves Congar, and Josef Geiselmann did the most work on the development of doctrine.

Rahner suggested that because revelation is divine communication, doctrine should develop in the history of the church—and not merely as a matter of making formally explicit what was formally implicit in the original deposit. Revelation conveys things "virtually" as well, which cannot be reduced to any final, finite form—any standard set of words—but are made more explicit over time under the guidance of the Spirit and the church. As a young man in love knows and feels many things too profound to be expressed in his early love letters, things communicated better over a steady course of time, so God shows himself to the bride of Christ, the church, who fathoms her Beloved—first revealed long ago—asymptotically through time. In the present life she always has room for improvement in her knowledge of the Lord. But the church's teaching office has "an organ of perception by which she can tell whether something which, from our point of view, emerges as a result of theological activity, is in fact objectively something more than the result of human speculation; whether it is still God's Word, though now expressed propositionally, in a new form, in a new articulation and explication."[64]

Congar, like Rahner, wrote frequently on Scripture, tradition, and the church, contending that the forces in this triad of authority always work together by the power of the Spirit. The Bible, he averred, is materially sufficient though formally insufficient for the church's

---

64. Karl Rahner, *Schriften Zur Theologie, I* (Einsiedeln: Benziger Verlag, 1954), chap. 3; trans., *Theological Investigations*, vol. 1, *God, Christ, Mary and Grace*, trans. Cornelius Ernst (Baltimore: Helicon Press, 1961), quotation from 75.

cardinal doctrines. The faithful had long enjoyed unwritten customs that enhanced their faith and practice. But everything essential to salvation is in Scripture, interpreted for them through tradition in the church. *Totum in scriptura, totum in traditione* ("all in Scripture, all in tradition"), Congar claimed with the likes of Cardinal Newman. These are never "to be placed side by side as rivals, but always to be combined, and referred each to each." When push came to shove, further, Scripture won pride of place in Congar's triad, worrying traditionalists within the Catholic Church. The Bible, tradition, and the church, he confessed, "are not on the same level." Rather, Scripture "has an absolute sovereignty; it is of divine origin, even in its literary form; it governs Tradition and the Church, whereas it is not governed by Tradition or by the Church."[65]

Geiselmann denied what is often called the "two-source theory" of authority in Catholic Church history, a theory usually said to have been formalized at Trent and then wielded to divide Roman Catholics and Protestants. He denied, more specifically, that hierarchs at Trent taught that Scripture and tradition stood as separate and parallel sources of authority. They had entertained this notion in the council's early stages but had ultimately decided, in Geiselmann's construction, that Scripture and tradition both offer God's Word to the faithful in the church—and do so together—*totum in scriptura, totum in traditione*. This implied that the Bible is materially sufficient for Christian dogmatics; it does not need supplements from unwritten sources (whose historicity was now difficult to prove). Academics tied to Tübingen, where Geiselmann taught on the theological faculty, were far more involved in higher-critical work on the Bible than most other Catholics, which complicated Geiselmann's reception in the Church and raised concern about the bearing of his work on

---

65. Yves M.-J. Congar, *La Tradition et les traditions*, vol. 1, *Essai historique*; vol. 2, *Essai théologique* (Paris: A. Fayard, 1960–63); trans. by Michael Naseby and Thomas Rainborough as *Tradition and Traditions: An Historical and a Theological Essay* (London: Burns & Oates, 1966), quotations from 414, 421–22.

Christian doctrine. But by the early 1960s, the bishops were abuzz about Scripture and tradition—and most would soon repudiate the two-source theory.[66]

These efforts to reevaluate the nature and history of doctrine and dynamics of tradition culminated at Vatican II (1962–65), the most influential council since the Reformation era. Its delegates did not contravene older teachings. But they did move past some medieval ways of speaking of our triad of authority—Scripture, tradition, and the church's teaching office—especially the suggestion that the Bible and tradition had been parallel sources of divine revelation whose interpretation by holy mother church was now fixed. In a document that changed the face of Protestant-Catholic dialogue, "Dogmatic Constitution on Divine Revelation," known best as *Dei Verbum*, the council fathers argued that the Bible and tradition intersect in their witness—forming a common fund of truth—and that the church makes progress in its teaching over time by the guidance of the Spirit. There is "growth in understanding of what is handed on," they claimed, "both the words and the realities they signify." Our sacred writings regulate the movement of tradition, while tradition regulates further study of the Bible. The kernel of this statement is worth quoting here at length:

> Tradition and scripture are bound together in a close and reciprocal relationship. They both flow from the same divine wellspring, merge together to some extent, and are on course towards the same end. Scripture is the utterance of God as it is set down in writing under the guidance of God's Spirit; tradition preserves the word of God as it was entrusted to the apostles by Christ our lord and the holy Spirit, and

66. Josef Rupert Geiselmann, *Die Heilige Schrift und die Tradition: Zu den neueren Kontroversen über das Verhältnis der Heiligen Schrift zu den nichtgeschriebenen Traditionen, Quaestiones Disputatae* (Freiburg im Breisgau: Herder, 1962), 91–107, 274–82, in keeping with the argument of Dutch church historian J. N. Bakhuizen van den Brink, *Traditio in de Reformatie en het Katholicisme in de zestiende eeuw*, Mededeelingen der Koninklijke Nederlandsche Akademie van Wetenschappen (Amsterdam: Noord-Hollandsche Uitgevers Maatschappij, 1952). Geiselmann had floated early versions of his thesis since the mid-1950s. Its publication in book form in 1962, though, caused quite a stir at the Second Vatican Council.

transmits it to their successors, so that these in turn, enlightened by the Spirit of truth, may faithfully preserve, expound and disseminate the word by their preaching. Consequently, the church's certainty about all that is revealed is not drawn from holy scripture alone; both scripture and tradition are to be accepted and honoured with like devotion and reverence. . . . Tradition and scripture together form a single sacred deposit of the word of God, entrusted to the church. . . . The task of authentically interpreting the word of God, whether in its written form or in that of tradition, has been entrusted only to those charged with the church's ongoing teaching function, whose authority is exercised in the name of Jesus Christ.[67]

As attested in the *Catechism of the Catholic Church* (1992), Vatican II is now the standard for discussions of our triad of authority in the Church. Planted deep in *Dei Verbum*, which it excerpts extensively, the *Catechism* teaches that the gospel of our Lord "was handed on in two ways," through Scripture and tradition, which together constitute one deposit of the faith. God's people ever plumb this deposit "more deeply," applying it "more fully," but "the task of interpreting" it "authentically," at least, "has been entrusted solely to the Magisterium of the Church, that is, to the Pope and to the bishops in communion with him."[68]

The most important Catholic commentator on Scripture, tradition, and the Spirit in the church since the end of Vatican II was Joseph Ratzinger, later Pope Benedict XVI. His work on Christian doctrine spanned four major seasons of his service to the church: that during Vatican II, his time as an exponent of the council after it ended, his ministry as Prefect of the Congregation for the Doctrine of the Faith (1981–2005), and his tenure in the papacy (2005–2013). Young

67. Second Vatican Council, session 8, November 18, 1965, in Tanner, *Decrees of the Ecumenical Councils*, 2:974–75.

68. *Catechismus Catholicae Ecclesiae*, part 1, section 1, article 2; trans., *Catechism of the Catholic Church, with Modification from the Editio Typica* (New York: Doubleday, 1995), 29–35, available at the Vatican website, http://www.vatican.va/archive/ENG0015/_INDEX.HTM.

Ratzinger labored as an "expert" (*peritus*) at Vatican II for Cardinal Josef Frings, Archbishop of Cologne, and played a crucial role assisting German delegates, especially, at work on *Dei Verbum*. In the wake of the council, he interpreted its judgments in a spate of publications. He became an archbishop in 1977. And in 1981, he was asked to lead the Church's most important teaching body, propagating its doctrine from the Vatican.

As Prefect of the Congregation for the Doctrine of the Faith, he addressed our concerns in several ad hoc speeches. Then in the most important book ever written on the subject, he presented his ideas in comprehensive fashion, anticipating statements he would make on the subject from the chair of Saint Peter. *God's Word: Scripture-Tradition-Office* did three things. (1) It repudiated the principle of *sola scriptura* and the material sufficiency of Scripture for dogmatics (contra Geiselmann et al.), noting that most Christians cherish doctrines not taken solely from the biblical materials—not even with the help of distinctions like those between virtual, formal, and material implications of the original deposit. (2) It said that council fathers at Trent had a capacious view of tradition, one that ought to be maintained by the Catholic Church today. This does not require access to unwritten customs understood as a material source of doctrine on their own. But it does call for faith in God speaking through tradition, which transcends and subsumes both Scripture and the church. "Revelation signifies all God's acts and utterances directed to man," in the Bible, the church, and the history of the world, "a *reality* of which Scripture gives us *information* but that *is* not simply Scripture itself," he explained. (3) It reiterated that bishops in communion with the pope—the Roman magisterium—are appointed and enabled by the Lord to hear his voice and define Christian doctrine for the faithful.[69]

---

69. Joseph Ratzinger [Pope Benedict XVI], *Wort Gottes: Schrift-Tradition-Amt* (Freiburg im Breisgau: Herder, 2005); trans., *God's Word: Scripture-Tradition-Office*, ed. Peter Hünermann and Thomas Söding (San Francisco: Ignatius, 2008), quotations from 51–53.

Shepherding the church left Benedict little opportunity for research or complex writing. But he did publish a major apostolic exhortation on our theme while pope, entitled *Verbum Domini* (2010), which codified the doctrine he had worked on for years and dispatched it to the world with the stamp of Saint Peter. Pope Benedict underscored two "essential" roles of tradition in this document (depicting tradition, again, as the source of both the canon and the teachings of the church): it helps Christians recognize the Bible as God's Word; and it helps them to grow in the knowledge of the same. "We see clearly, then," he reasoned, "how important it is for the People of God to be properly taught and trained to approach the sacred Scriptures in relation to the Church's living Tradition." As they do so, he summarized, "the Church hands on to every generation all that has been revealed in Christ. The Church lives in the certainty that her Lord, who spoke in the past, continues today to communicate his word in her living Tradition and in sacred Scripture. Indeed," he went on in what had become his usual fashion, "the word of God is given to us in sacred Scripture as an inspired testimony to revelation; together with the Church's living Tradition, it constitutes the supreme rule of faith."[70]

Roman Catholics are not the only ones to rethink the Spirit's role in guiding Christian teaching since the end of Vatican II. A vast array of Christians has engaged this concern. I will pay greater attention to their views in chapter 3, where I survey contemporary approaches to the nature and development of doctrine. For now, a brief sampling of their work must suffice, one that focuses more closely on the relationship of Scripture and tradition in the church than on the leading theories of doctrine, its purposes, and its roles.

Among the Orthodox, the Ukrainian-Russian priest Georges Florovsky, who taught in Paris and the United States, has done the most

---

70. Benedict XVI, *Verbum Domini: On the Word of God in the Life and Mission of the Church* (2010), §§17–18, available at the Vatican website, http://w2.vatican.va/content/benedict-xvi/en /apost_exhortations/documents/hf_ben-xvi_exh_20100930_verbum-domini.html.

important work on Scripture and tradition. Along with Orthodox colleagues such as Vladimir Lossky, Sergei Bulgakov, and Dumitru Stăniloae (a Romanian), he contended that the faith and worship of the people of God is the treasury of tradition and that the fathers—more than popes, church councils, and academics—are the most important guides to what the Spirit says in Scripture. In a series of publications gathered in 1972, he wrote, "Opinions of the Fathers and of the ecumenical Doctors of the Church frequently have greater spiritual value and finality than the definitions of certain councils. And these opinions do not need to be verified and accepted by 'universal consent'" (*pace* Vincent of Lérins). The seven great councils are authoritative, of course. But the "'Fathers' were those who transmitted and propagated the right doctrine, the teaching of the Apostles, who were guides and masters in Christian instruction and catechesis." As he put this in reference to the Bible and the church,

> It must be kept in mind that the main, if not also the only, manual of faith and doctrine was, in the Ancient Church, precisely the Holy Writ. And for that reason the renowned interpreters of Scripture were regarded as "Fathers" in an eminent sense. . . . Two major points must be made in this connection: *First*, the phrase "the Fathers of the Church" has actually an obvious *restrictive* accent: they were acting not just as individuals, but rather as *viri ecclesiastici* [church representatives]. . . . *Secondly*, it was precisely the *consensus patrum* [consensus of the fathers] which was authoritative and binding, and not their private opinions or views, although even they should not be hastily dismissed.[71]

The Spirit led the fathers in the exegesis of Scripture, and the fathers, as an ancient, magisterial consortium, shaped the worship, faith, and practice of the rest of God's people, including church officials—and should do so today.

71. Georges Florovsky, *Bible, Church, Tradition: An Eastern Orthodox View*, in *The Collected Works of Georges Florovsky* (Belmont, MA: Nordland, 1972), 1:51–54.

Several Protestants have also penned influential texts on these themes since Vatican II. The Anglican Richard Bauckham has contended in the face of liberal Protestants and forward-leaning Catholic leaders alike that the Bible "is not simply the first part of the tradition." Rather, "the church's recognition of the canon of Scripture created a real break, which gave the origin of the tradition, in this written form, a uniquely normative status in relation to the rest." Interpreters of Scripture ought to learn from the past. But their teaching should not be a top-down affair. The development of doctrine is "the generation of fresh meaning in the encounter between Scripture and new contexts," he claims, a meaning that is stunted and sometimes even spoiled when restrained by tradition or contained from above.[72]

The Scottish Methodist I. Howard Marshall has proposed that the New Testament authors handled Old Testament texts, the ministry of Jesus, and apostolic writings in a way that yields guidelines for teachers in the present. They did not view "individual texts as units of meaning" but saw them as parts of an ongoing story of redemption. They read texts, that is, not in isolated bits, with meanings ever fixed, but as part of God's saving work continuing today. Some texts "may be seen," then, "as staging posts on the way to fuller understanding; they are no longer valid in their original form . . . but continue to be authoritative in a different way." Divine teaching progressed over the course of the canon, so "developments in doctrine and new understandings after the closing of the canon are inevitable," he reasons.[73]

The American evangelical Kevin J. Vanhoozer has revised Marshall's plan for the development of doctrine. "We move from Bible to doctrine," he has written in response, not by wielding general principles for moving past its teachings derived anachronistically from what some believe to be its sacred hermeneutic, "but rather by discerning

72. Richard Bauckham, "Tradition in Relation to Scripture and Reason," in *Scripture, Tradition, and Reason: A Study in the Criteria of Christian Doctrine; Essays in Honour of Richard P. C. Hanson*, ed. Richard Bauckham and Benjamin Drewery (Edinburgh: T&T Clark, 1988), 127–29, 145.

73. I. Howard Marshall, *Beyond the Bible: Moving from Scripture to Theology*, Acadia Studies in Bible and Theology (Grand Rapids: Baker Academic, 2004), 78–79.

and continuing a pattern of judgment" that recurs in the canon in
many forms. The Bible yields guidelines for handing on the faith; but
expositors must not contradict what it says in the name of forward
progress. They must learn, rather, to "render the same kind of judgments as those embedded in the canon in new contexts and with
different concepts."[74] As Vanhoozer has recapitulated this argument
more recently, "the development of doctrine is a matter of thinking
biblically in new situations. Scripture shapes our vision of the whole,
instills mental habits, forms the desire of our hearts, and trains us
in the way of discipleship. . . . Doctrinal development is ultimately
a matter of the church's faith improvisation in accordance with the
Scriptures and with earlier faithful improvisations."[75]

Perhaps most importantly, majority-world leaders have proposed
new approaches to our subject since Vatican II, attracting more attention from their colleagues in the West than at any time since 1054.
Many underscore the notion that "the Word of God grew" (or "increased," or "advanced") as the early church spread in the Lukan
book of Acts (ὁ λόγος τοῦ θεοῦ ηὔξανεν [Acts 6:7; 12:24; 19:20]).
In the West, this phrase is usually said to have referred to numerical
expansion by means of Christian witness. But global Christians often
say the faith itself grew—that Christian doctrine grew—as the Word
was embraced in new cultural situations. As the Gambian Catholic
thinker Lamin Sanneh has reminded us, "Christianity is a translated
religion because the Gospels themselves were a translated version of
the preaching of Jesus [from Aramaic to Greek], and . . . the missionary milieu of the early church necessitated further translations and, by
implication, fresh adaptations of the faith." Christianity, he stresses,
"is not intrinsically a religion of cultural uniformity"; it is a religion

---

74. Kevin J. Vanhoozer, "Into the Great 'Beyond': A Theologian's Response to the Marshall
Plan," in Marshall, *Beyond the Bible*, 93.
75. Vanhoozer, "Improvising Theology according to the Scriptures: An Evangelical Account
of the Development of Doctrine," in *Building on the Foundations of Evangelical Theology: Essays
in Honor of John S. Feinberg*, ed. Gregg R. Allison and Stephen J. Wellum (Wheaton: Crossway,
2015), 44–45.

of translatability. "More people pray and worship in more languages in Christianity than in any other religion in the world," he reports. This cultural malleability, moreover, bears crucial implications for the teaching of the faith in the church. "There must be wider benefits for all in the movements of renewal taking place in a post-Western world Christianity," he claims.

> The tradition of exegesis that has been practiced in the West seems to have run its course. There are too many instances of recycling and cultural discounting, and too willing a tendency to suppress difference, for us not to think that the envelope can't be pushed much further. The standard exegesis spins faith into just more cultural filibuster. Yet in Africa and elsewhere there is enough sense of commodiousness, with fresh materials being introduced into Scripture, prayers, hymns, and liturgy, for that not to affect how people in the West think and speak about the gospel and the church.[76]

As we will see in chapter 2, postcolonial endeavors to contextualize the faith, or indigenize doctrine, are affecting catechesis all over the Christian world. In many different churches, especially those with a modicum of missionary verve and ecumenical awareness, ordinary Christians are advancing in discipleship in ways shaped profoundly by those outside the West. The future volume of this project will reflect this trend, demonstrating clearly that handing on the faith has been an international enterprise for two thousand years. For now, I note simply that this ministry continues, facilitated afresh by the forces of globalization. Japanese theologians are changing the way we understand the suffering of God in the person of Jesus Christ. South Africans are changing what we say about the Spirit. Argentineans are changing what we teach about the gospel, encouraging an accent on good news for the poor. This list could be extended for a very long time. Even the

---

76. Lamin Sanneh, *Whose Religion Is Christianity? The Gospel beyond the West* (Grand Rapids: Eerdmans, 2003), 129–30, 69, 58–59.

most conservative teachers in most denominations now believe that Christian doctrine can develop for the better and that non-Western Christians have much to teach us all. In this era of improvement, they are listening to the Spirit with a new sort of intensity, hoping he will guide them as they live by the Word in a complicated, frightening, and ever-changing world.

The Spirit-Bound Body of Christ as "Pillar" and "Bulwark" of Christian Teaching

As I hope is clear by now, Christians have toiled through two thousand years of disagreement over how best to teach about the faith in congregations. Tracking with the Spirit as he leads us into truth has proven harder than it seems, even with a canon of Scripture and a long-standing history of interpretation behind it. Teaching in, with, and under the Christian church has been contentious, even when our leaders shared structures of authority. Most have concurred with the Lord's apostle John: "the Spirit is the one" who "testifies" to the truth. If "we receive human testimony, the testimony of God is greater." And "those who believe in the Son of God have the testimony in their hearts" (1 John 5:6–10). Finding language, though, for what is in the heart can be mysterious. Putting words to our faith in Jesus Christ can be a challenge. Not many should be teachers, as James the Just warned, "for you know that we who teach will be judged with greater strictness" (James 3:1). Hence those who seek to teach in the service of the church—transmitting Christian faith, indeed handling sacred truth—without recourse to the history of the church's teaching ministry are naïve at best, blatantly negligent at worst. There are answers we can live by to the questions raised here about inculcating doctrine, and about the roles of the Bible and tradition in so doing. But we need to understand them. And people who neglect the tradition of debate about the sources of our teaching will not even understand the questions.

The stakes of pedagogical improvement are high. As Paul challenged the Ephesians, the church of Christ is one, and its witness should be unified. "[Bear] with one another in love," he urged them, "making every effort to maintain the unity of the Spirit in the bond of peace. There is one body and one Spirit," he added theologically, "just as you were called to the one hope of your calling, one Lord, one faith, one baptism, one God and Father of all, who is above all and through all and in all" (Eph. 4:2–6). Such unity implies—and requires—a common core to the faith we deliver to disciples in the church. And this core should represent, inspire, and facilitate our union with the Lord and profession to the world. As Jesus asked the Father, "May [they] all be one. As you, Father, are in me and I am in you, may they also be in us, so that the world may believe that you have sent me. The glory that you have given me I have given them, so that they may be one, as we are one, I in them and you in me, that they may become completely one, so that the world may know that you have sent me and have loved them even as you have loved me" (John 17:21–23). Does our teaching serve the ends to which the Lord Jesus prayed?

Despite our disagreements and their bearing on our testimony, the members of the church of Christ have transcendent reason and support for perseverance. The communion of the saints is an ancient, immense, highly variegated fellowship. But those who bear the Spirit are united with the Lord—and, in him, with one another—and have everything they need to give voice to the faith. As Paul encouraged his younger charge Timothy in Ephesus, shoring up his confidence and strengthening his witness, "the household of God," the "church of the living God," is now and ever shall be a divinely anchored "pillar and bulwark of the truth" (1 Tim. 3:14–15). She represents her Lord as the temple of his Spirit, an indefectible witness to the truth and potential of his everlasting Word.

2

From Every Tribe and Language

Then I saw between the throne and the four living creatures and among the elders a Lamb standing as if it had been slaughtered, having seven horns and seven eyes, which are the seven spirits of God sent out into all the earth. He went and took the scroll from the right hand of the one who was seated on the throne. When he had taken the scroll, the four living creatures and the twenty-four elders fell before the Lamb, each holding a harp and golden bowls full of incense, which are the prayers of the saints. They sing a new song: "You are worthy to take the scroll and to open its seals, for you were slaughtered and by your blood you ransomed for God saints from every tribe and language and people and nation; you have made them to be a kingdom and priests serving our God, and they will reign on the earth."

—Revelation 5:6–10

The global composition of the church of Jesus Christ has long fortified its power as a "pillar" of the truth, much as steel's composite character enhances tensile strength and increases its capacity to bear heavy loads. The sending of the Spirit I discussed in chapter 1 led not only to the doctrines that we teach in the churches, and not only to the growth of the worldwide family of God. It united God's family across racial and ethnic lines, strengthening our witness to the gospel of the Lord and ability to teach the Christian faith with comprehension.

Ever since the call of Abram—right after the fall of Babel in the story line of Genesis, redeeming the nations that had just been dispersed— God has promised to provide for "all the families of the earth" in his plan of salvation (Gen. 12:3; cf. Gal. 3:8). He repeated this pledge to Abram's grandson Jacob when establishing the land later given to the Jews (Gen. 28:14). He expanded on it frequently in Old Testament prophecy (e.g., Pss. 2:6–8; 22:27–28; Isa. 24:14–16; 42:10–12; 49:5–6; Zech. 2:11; 8:20–23; 14:16; Mal. 1:11). He even planted gentiles such as Rahab and Ruth in the lineage of Jesus. The Gospels and Epistles chart the spread of God's kingdom well beyond the promised land. The Acts of the Apostles features missionary work among gentile converts. Paul announces their inclusion in "the household of God" (Eph. 2:19). And the Apocalypse of John shows that all of this will climax at the end of mundane history in the coming new Jerusalem. "The nations will walk by its light," John declares of this diverse, heavenly city, "and the kings of the earth will bring their glory into it. Its gates will never be shut by day—and there will be no night there. People will bring into it the glory and the honour of the nations" (Rev. 21:24–26).

This multinational makeup has attracted unprecedented attention in recent years (though all too often without the four thousand years of history behind it). The rapid, recent growth of Christianity in Africa, China, and other parts of South and East Asia; the rise of Christian missions to the West from such places; the spread of multilateralism in denominational enterprises, parachurch leadership, and Christian education (at least in fits and starts)—not to mention independence movements in many former colonies with Christian populations, the decolonization of their churches and ministries, new patterns of migration among believers seeking better opportunities abroad, and the impact of globalism and theories of globalization in economics, technology, entertainment, the professions, the arts, and foreign policy—have boosted our awareness of the church's international constitution like never before in history.

The church has almost always been an international family, though. Our numbers have grown since the early modern period, especially in places now labeled "global south." But our multicultural character is not a new invention. And false impressions about our past can distort Christian doctrine. (The technology through which we see the world, of course, is new, which can make what we see appear more novel than it is.) In the rest of this chapter, then, I narrate the emergence of the notion of the global south in modern church history, remind us that the church has always proven cosmopolitan (relatively speaking, with undeniable expansion in the seventeenth, eighteenth, and nineteenth centuries—and then again during and after the last third of the twentieth century), emphasize the difference this has made in our teaching, and discuss both the promise and the peril of more recent postcolonial, "non-Western Christianities" for handing on the faith in a world more focused on diversity and self-determination than tradition.

Modern Missions, Western Power, and the Rise of "the Global South"

Devoted disciples of Christ have engaged in Christian mission since the day of Pentecost. Soon after the resurrection and before his ascension, Jesus met the Eleven on a hillside in Galilee. "All authority in heaven and on earth has been given to me," he told them in a statement now called the Great Commission. "Go therefore and make disciples of all nations, baptizing them in the name of the Father and of the Son and of the Holy Spirit, and teaching them to obey everything that I have commanded you" (Matt. 28:18–20). He ordered them to wait in Jerusalem a while for "the promise of the Father." When the Spirit comes "upon you," he explained this promise, "you will be my witnesses in Jerusalem, in all Judea and Samaria, and to the ends of the earth" (Acts 1:4–8). As noted in chapter 1, God's Spirit did arrive, and these missionaries witnessed to the Lord among the nations. "Are not all these who are speaking Galileans?" some asked about their unlettered messengers on Pentecost morning. "How is it that we hear, each of us, in our own native language? Parthians, Medes, Elamites, and residents of Mesopotamia, Judea and Cappadocia, Pontus and Asia, Phrygia and Pamphylia, Egypt and the parts of Libya belonging to Cyrene, and visitors from Rome, both Jews and proselytes, Cretans and Arabs—in our own languages we hear them speaking about God's deeds of power" (Acts 2:7–11). This testimony multiplied through early church history, as witnessed in the rest of the apostolic writings and other ancient materials. I will summarize the spread of Christianity below. For now, I note simply that though estimates of ancient Christian growth rates vary (and are not scientific), even the most cautious scholars place the number of disciples by the year 150 at about forty thousand, by the year 200 over two hundred thousand, and by the year 300 in excess of six million. The Spirit raised disciples who equipped more disciples—a few of whom traveled "to the ends of the earth"—accelerating the growth of the church for years to come.

Something special happened, though, in the early modern period, confounding those accustomed to the church's usual growth rates and creating what many now call the global south (a Western view of others made possible by modern technology, the media, and massive generalization). European trade and exploration overseas factored into this phenomenon, as did noteworthy spikes in Europe's Christian population. But efforts to renew the state churches of the West, which, in turn, yielded what we call the modern missions movement, took the lead in a story of exceptional expansion. Extraordinary numbers swelled the ranks of foreign missions, undergirded by a burgeoning evangelistic network. Tens of thousands of disciples now evangelized the nations. By 1900, the worldwide Christian church topped six hundred million, nearly 35 percent of the global population. Many thought the next century would be "the Christian century," a golden age of world Christianity.

During the so-called Middle Ages the geography of Christendom had contracted severely, due in no small measure to the conquests of Islam. Though centered in West Asia for its first several centuries—with major populations in North Africa, Europe, and South and Central Asia—Christian territory had shrunk, by 1500, to a shadow of its former self. A thousand years before (in the year 500), it comprised one-fifth of the global population and was centered demographically in the eastern Mediterranean. Now it comprised a smaller portion of the race (17.9 percent)—even the total number of Christians had declined since 1300, by nearly 10 percent—and its global center of gravity was in the heart of Europe. Nearly 92 percent of Christians now lived in Europe—a remarkable statistic—more than ever before or since. A small fraction still inhabited the Middle East and Asia (mostly Orthodox, Thomas, and Nestorian believers) and parts of northern Africa (mostly Copts, Ethiopians, and widely scattered Nubians). But many Christian leaders now felt a sense of urgency to grow the church again and redeem the world for Christ. Roman Catholics took the lead, primarily by colonizing territory abroad—in what became Latin America, Africa, and Asia—and usually through the ministries of missionary orders: Augustinians, Dominicans, Franciscans, their Capuchin descendants, and especially the Jesuits.[1]

The most famous—and notorious—early modern Catholic missions took place in the Americas. From the late fifteenth century to the early nineteenth century, the Spanish and the Portuguese conquered and colonized the peoples of the Caribbean, Mesoamerica, and regions to the south (most notably Peru), disseminating faith by the power of the sword. Christopher Columbus, a devout Italian Catholic paid to sail for the Spanish, sought a maritime route to what he called the

---

1. Statistics from Todd M. Johnson and Sun Young Chung, "Christianity's Centre of Gravity, AD 33–2100," in *Atlas of Global Christianity, 1910–2010*, ed. Todd M. Johnson and Kenneth R. Ross (Edinburgh: Edinburgh University Press, 2009), 50–53.

"east Indies" (South and Southeast Asia, where Europeans traded), but settled for a beachhead in the future "west Indies." An amateur divine, he said his number one goal was to spread the Christian gospel. With millennial aspiration, he took a Hebrew interpreter in 1492, just in case the natives really were a remnant of the ten lost tribes of ancient Israel. On October 12, he rowed ashore an island in the Bahamas, named it after Jesus (*San Salvador*, "holy Savior"), planted a cross and a flag, and claimed its land for Catholic Spain. In the decades that followed, Hernan Cortés, Francisco Pizarro, and thousands more conquistadors commandeered the land and natural riches of the "new world," Christianizing the continent with ruthless efficiency. The Spanish and the Portuguese, competing for position in this missionary venture, asked the pope to intervene and split the continent between them. Thus Alexander VI drew a line down the globe, giving Spain the right to colonize the regions to its west and Portugal the options on the lands to the east. He had to shift the line westward as explorers learned the continent was wider than they thought. His division was affirmed in the Treaty of Tordesillas (1494). Consequently, the Spanish took most of Latin America while the Portuguese colonized the coastal regions of Africa, India, and several parts of Asia.

During the sixteenth century Spanish missionaries went to what later became the United States, but they met stiff resistance from the regional inhabitants and made fewer converts than they had to the south. Juan Ponce de León led the first known European expedition to Florida. He disembarked at what he christened *La Florida* on Easter Sunday 1513, naming it after *Pascua Florida*, the "Easter feast of flowers." Pedro Menéndez de Avilés established the first lasting Catholic outpost in the United States, St. Augustine, Florida, in 1565, taking a Spanish priest with him (Francisco López de Mendoza Grajales), facilitating Masses, killing nearby Huguenots, and founding a mission. It was in the southwest of what became the United States, though, that Spaniards did the most for their nation and its church. In 1598, four hundred of their pioneers traveled to New Mexico with eight

Franciscan missionaries. They settled near the Rio Grande, north of El Paso, building churches and the largest and most durable Spanish settlement in modern-day America. During the eighteenth century, Franciscans like Junípero Serra spread the gospel up the country's west coast. They raised twenty-one missions in what is now California, the first in San Diego in 1769. However, nonmonastic missions proved rare and short-lived. As late as 1836, only two secular priests lived and ministered in Texas. In 1840, there were none in what is now California. And in 1846, there were none in Arizona.

By the late nineteenth century, most of the "new world" south of the twenty-eighth parallel north of the equator (the line traveled by Columbus) had become Roman Catholic—at least in name, often in fact. But the road to Christianization had been paved with destruction, leaving present-day Christians with a shameful inheritance. According to the first priest ordained in the Western Hemisphere, Bartolomé de Las Casas, a Dominican acclaimed the "apostle of the Indies," conquistador religion was a devilish affair. In *The Destruction of the Indies* (1552), a blistering attack on his fellow Spanish Christians, he lashed out at those who evangelized with cruelty. "The Spaniards first assaulted the innocent Sheep," he reported, "like most cruel Tygers, Wolves and Lions hunger-starv'd." Their raping and stealing had begun off shore—on the Caribbean islands—but overwhelmed the continent in less than half a century. "As to the firm land [the continent], we are certainly . . . assur'd, that the Spaniards by their barbarous and execrable Actions have absolutely depopulated Ten Kingdoms, of greater extent than all Spain, . . . above One Thousand Miles, which now lye wast and desolate." Many millions lost their lives. "And so solicitous" were the Christians of the inhabitants' spiritual condition "that the above-mentioned number of People died without understanding the true Faith or Sacraments. . . . I desire therefore," Las Casas admonished, "that the Readers who have or shall peruse these passages, would please seriously to consider whether or no, such Barbarous, Cruel and Inhumane Acts as these do not transcend and exceed all the impiety and tyrany, which can enter into the thoughts or imagination of Man, and whether these Spaniards deserve not the name of Devils. For which of these two things is more eligible or desirable," he challenged his compatriots, "whether the Indians should be delivered up to the Devils themselves to be tormented or the Spaniards? That is still a question."[2]

Many other Catholic missions stemmed from colonizing ventures—or commercial interventions in non-Western economies—but some bore fruit that was not quite so bitter. Those performed by the Society of Jesus, in particular, often proved to be more culturally adept and benign. The most important missionaries of the early modern period, the Society (usually known by its nickname, the Jesuits) arose when a nobleman and former Spanish soldier named Ignatius of Loyola, a profound spiritual writer, led six of his friends in vows of poverty, chastity, and usefulness to God (1534). Though they lived then in Paris, they aspired to go to Palestine as missionaries to Muslims. They rode first to Venice, seeking passage to the Holy Land, but danger on the high seas inhibited their progress (1537). They had pledged to go to Rome if their first hope failed, presenting their now growing congregation to the pope and agreeing to perform whatever tasks he required "for the greater glory of God" (*ad majorem Dei gloriam*, the motto of the Jesuits). And this is what they did. Pope Paul III approved them as an order of the Catholic Church (1540). The Jesuits submitted all they had to the papacy. They distinguished themselves as foreign missionaries, teachers, and apologists for Rome. And by 1556 (the year Ignatius died), they had a thousand members, many of whom served the church as ministers abroad.

The most revered Jesuit missionary was Francis Xavier, a lieutenant of Loyola named "apostle of the Indies" (like Las Casas before him) and, in 1927, copatron of foreign missions for the Roman Catholic

2. Bartolomé de Las Casas, *Brevísima relación de la destrucción de las Indias* (Seville: Sebastian Trugillo, 1552); trans. (unpaginated) at Project Gutenberg, http://www.gutenberg.org/cache/epub /20321/pg20321-images.html.

Church. Under the sponsorship of King João (John) III of Portugal, he journeyed south to India in 1541 to serve and edify colonists (his remit from the king) and evangelize natives (his primary passion). He preached for three years in southern India and Sri Lanka, converting many locals and founding forty churches. Then in 1545, he set sail to the east, trailblazing as a missionary in Southeast Asia. He stopped first in Malacca, a Portuguese colony in present-day Malaysia, where he taught a few months. Then he traveled through several of the Maluku Islands (in today's Indonesia) where the Portuguese had settled. He became the first missionary to serve in Japan (in 1549). He struggled with the language and encountered opposition but managed to prepare a way for Jesuit successors. After touching base in India in 1552, he secured a ship to China in the spring of that year. Landing first on an island southwest of Macau—called São João in Portuguese, Saint John in English, and Shangchuan in Chinese—he died of a fever while seeking transport to the mainland. Though his body has been moved (it now rests in Goa Velha, on the southwest coast of India), a Xavier Tomb Monument and Chapel draws tourists to the Shangchuan Island yet today.

The most controversial missionary from early modern Europe was a Jesuit from the Papal States (in modern-day Italy), Matteo Ricci, who traveled in Xavier's wake for nearly thirty years. Leaving Lisbon for India in 1578, he labored in Goa (Asia's first Catholic diocese) until 1582, when he journeyed to Macau (another Portuguese colony) in the hope of reaching China. One of the first Western missionaries to master Chinese, he made it to the mainland in 1583, where he settled in Zhaoqing until 1589. Admired for his learning, he drew maps, taught math, and compiled the first Portuguese-Chinese dictionary (with the help of a partner, Pompilio Ruggieri) before regional authorities requested that he leave. He went to several other cities and, in 1601, settled down in Beijing as an advisor to the court of the Wanli Emperor—the first European to gain entrance to the grounds of the Forbidden City. He evangelized several leading Chinese courtiers, some of whom converted; established the Cathedral of the Immaculate Conception; and continued to collaborate with China's best and brightest in astronomy, cartography, and other forms of learning. He adopted the culture of traditional Confucianism, mimicked the manners of the local literati, and dressed in the fashion of the scholarly elite. He used Chinese concepts to explain Christianity, sanctioned Confucian-style ancestor worship (a controversial move among Christians ever since), and suggested that the Christian faith was not a foreign import but a supplement and crown of Chinese culture. So respected was Ricci by imperial officials that, when he died in 1610, an exception was approved—and a Buddhist temple built—so his body could be buried in Beijing.

Even in the Americas, the Jesuits proved to be unusually sensitive missionaries, wielding gentler weapons in their battle for the faith. From the early seventeenth century, when the French began to colonize in present-day Canada, to the 1760s, when France and several other states suppressed their activity (for fear of their international strength and ties to Rome), the Society of Jesus moved with traders, fur trappers, and nomadic native tribes, assimilating to local ways of living as they went. Jacques Marquette, the most storied of these peripatetic priests, spent the bulk of his ministry in motion in the wilderness, often by canoe, evangelizing the natives of the upper Midwest of what became the United States. And Jean de Brébeuf, another Jesuit exemplar, toiled for two years without a single native convert, refusing to impose his faith on others by force. He left the comforts of Europe as he turned thirty-two (1625) and spent years by himself among the Hurons especially (in the northern Great Lakes), struggling with their language and adapting to their culture—in spite of racist views about their "savage" way of life—before seeing much success. Eventually, he supervised two different missions. But in 1649, he was captured by the Iroquois, tortured, and killed (along with many Hurons). His missionary methods netted far fewer converts than were boasted by the Spanish, but accrued less shame to his legacy as well.

Catholic missions grew so popular by 1622 that the Vatican decided to support and control them. Pope Gregory XV, a student of the Jesuits who canonized Ignatius of Loyola and Francis Xavier, erected what he called the Congregation for the Propagation of the Faith at the outset of his short-lived papacy (in Latin, Congregatio de Propaganda Fide). It organized and regulated all Catholic missions, housed a polyglot printing press, published Catholic teaching aids in many different languages, competed with the ministries of Protestants abroad, and established a missionary-training university (Pontificio Collegio Urbano de Propaganda Fide, or Pontifical Urban College for the Propagation of the Faith, built in 1627 by Pope Urban VIII, Pope Gregory's successor, and called Pontifical Urban University today). The Congregation facilitated the growth of Catholic missions like nothing else in history. In 1967, Pope Paul VI changed its name to the Congregation for the Evangelization of Peoples (Congregatio pro Gentium Evangelizatione).

Europe's Protestants lagged behind Rome in world missions. In the age of Martin Luther, they conceived of their reform as an effort to promote true faith on the earth in preparation for the second coming of Christ. Some believed the end was near and that the role of earnest Christians was to purify the church, restore its apostolic teaching, proclaim the gospel fearlessly, and resist the final ravages of sin, death, and the devil. They evangelized others as they carried out these tasks, and they eventually engaged in culture wars and culture making. But even after they lent support to officially Protestant governments— investing for the long haul—their state-church leaders usually spread the Christian faith in the manner of what scholars now call confessionalization. They inculcated doctrine as a means of edification and Christian nation building more than missionary training. Through teaching, the arts, visitation, and church discipline, they catechized the newly Protestant provinces of Europe, helping neighbors, first and foremost, in the practice of the faith. They had precious little awareness of—and even less capacity to sponsor—gospel ministry beyond their own borders. And a few within their ranks claimed the great commission obligated only the apostles, that God had chosen to grow his family after the apostolic era through organic, institutional development.

This is not to say, however, that they neglected cross-cultural evangelism completely. By the mid-1550s, Protestants like Calvin sent clergy to Brazil, most notably the Huguenot explorer Jean de Léry, who wrote about his journey after moving back to France (*History of a Voyage to the Land of Brazil*, 1578).[3] By 1559, Swedes were laboring in Lapland. In the early seventeenth century, Dutch and English trading firms staffed their colonies with clergy (though primarily to serve other European colonists). A German Lutheran pastor, Peter Heyling, sailed to Egypt in 1632, and then moved to Ethiopia in 1634, where he worked as a preacher with the region's Coptic Christians while serving as a doctor in the court of King Fasiladas. The Dutch Reformed did missions work in several different colonies—Formosa (now Taiwan), Indonesia, Ceylon (now Sri Lanka), Brazil, and elsewhere—during the seventeenth century. Gijsbert Voet, one of their most influential theologians, wrote the first major missiological work by a Protestant.[4] Great Britain's Lord Protector, Oliver Cromwell, devised an abortive educational institution for missionaries—to rival that in Rome—during the Puritan Interregnum. The Quakers launched missions in the late seventeenth century in places like Jerusalem and Constantinople. And by 1700, the Anglicans had funded foreign missions organizations that exist to this day: the Society for Promoting Christian Knowledge (1698) and the Society for the Propagation of the Gospel in Foreign Parts (1701).

Notwithstanding these beginnings, it would take another century— and leadership from state-church Protestant purveyors of revival and

---

3. Jean de Léry, *Histoire d'un voyage fait en la terre de Brésil*... (Rochelle: Antoine Chuppin, 1578), available at The Renaissance in Print, https://www.lib.virginia.edu/rmds/collections/gordon/travel/lery.html.

4. See especially Gisbertus Voetius, *Selectarum Disputationum Theologicarum...*, 5 vols. (Utrecht: Joannem à Waesberge, 1648–69); Voetius, *Politicae Ecclesiasticae*, 3 vols. (Amsterdam: Joannis à Waesberge, 1663–76).

renewal, like the Puritans and Pietists—before the world witnessed exponential Christian growth on the scale and in the manner of the modern missions movement (a title usually associated with Protestant endeavors). For not until the Puritans determined to evangelize New England's native people did the Protestants project such a grand foreign mission. And not until the Pietists evangelized others in a pan-ethnic, continental, ecumenical manner—without representing any territorial interests—did the Protestants enjoy much success overseas.

The Massachusetts Puritans professed in their charter that evangelizing natives was the "principall Ende" of their venture.[5] They nursed a love for souls, and, like Columbus before them, some wondered if the Indians descended from the ten lost tribes of ancient Israel, in which case their conversion was a necessary phase of the "grafting in" of Israel—or salvation of the Jews—on the eve of Christ's return (Rom. 11:11–36). With millennial expectation, then, they witnessed to their neighbors shortly after they arrived. They did not mount a massive campaign for native souls. But they did start evangelistic work in several places. In the 1640s, Thomas Mayhew the Younger began to serve on Martha's Vineyard (his father was the governor), pastoring the English and the native Pokanokets, establishing a school for the Pokanoket children, and converting nearly three hundred people in the process. At about the same time, John Eliot, the so-called "Apostle to the Indians," evangelized those on the Massachusetts mainland. He offered them the gospel, translated Scripture into the Massachusett language (also called Wampanoag or, by natives, Wôpanâak)—publishing the first whole Bible in the Americas with help from local tribesmen—and founded "praying towns" in which his protégés farmed, traded goods with the English, and grew in Christian faith.

By 1675, there were nearly five thousand "praying Indians" in New England. Still, many have contended that the Puritans fell short of their avowed "principall Ende," a sign of rank hypocrisy. A scion of

---

5. The Massachusetts Bay charter (1629) is available at the Avalon Project, Yale Law School, http://avalon.law.yale.edu/17th_century/mass03.asp.

their tribe, Solomon Stoddard, wrung his hands several decades after the Massachusetts charter had been signed:

> There has been a neglect to bring the Indians to the Profession of the Gospel. Something has been done through the Piety of particular Men, and at the Cost of some in Old-England; But we are reproached abroad for our Negligence. Many Men have been more careful to make a Prey of them, than to gain them to the Knowledge of Christ. The King in the CHARTER says, that the Undertakers did profess it to be their principal design to bring the Natives to the Knowledge of GOD. But we have very much failed of prosecuting that Design to Effect. . . . We have reason to fear that we are much to blame for their continuance in their Heathenism.[6]

Stoddard wondered aloud "whether God is not angry with the country for doing so little towards the conversion of the Indians."[7] By the early eighteenth century, many others wondered too—and a few burned with shame about the treatment of Indians by other English Christians. On top of shady business deals and spiritual neglect, Anglo-Indian relations had been riddled with contention and outright hostility. Tens of thousands of Native Americans died of English illnesses, sanctions, and wars, most shamefully King Philip's War, which decimated nearly all the Wampanoag nation (1675–76). And several hundred others— Indian men, women, and children—were enslaved near and far.

The Pietists' missions proved rather more successful, and nowhere near as deadly, as the Puritan attempts. Beyond their well-known ministries in several parts of Europe, they sent about sixty from their headquarters in Halle to non-Christian lands. Their most celebrated work was conceived in the heart of the Lutheran king of Denmark. Frederick IV hoped to bless his Christian colony of Tranquebar

---

6. Solomon Stoddard, *An Answer to Some Cases of Conscience, respecting the Country* (Boston: Green, 1722), 11–12.

7. Solomon Stoddard, *Whether God Is Not Angry for Doing So Little towards the Conversion of the Indians?* (Boston: Green, 1723), 6.

(spelled Trankebar in Danish, on the southeastern coast of the Indian subcontinent, today's Tharangambadi) with ardent gospel witness. Unable to secure Danish clergy for the job, he resorted—at the urging of his German court chaplain—to August Hermann Francke, Halle's leading gospel light. In 1706, two young Halle Pietists, Bartholomäus Ziegenbalg and Heinrich Plütschau, both protégés of Francke, began to preach at the outpost. The Society for Promoting Christian Knowledge lent them aid, as did Cotton Mather of Boston, a correspondent of Francke with a passion for evangelism. The Tranquebar mission soon became the most fruitful evangelical concern in all of Asia.

More crucial to the rise of modern evangelical missions, the Moravians sent hundreds of evangelists abroad. Descendants of the Hussites of Moravia/Bohemia (the Unitas Fratrum, or Unity of the Brethren), refugee Protestants from other parts of Europe, and Pietists from Halle, by the late 1720s they had come into their own on the Berthelsdorf estate of Count Nicholas von Zinzendorf (in present-day Saxony). They deemed themselves an independent, international movement—one that represented Christ, not a territorial church—and sent a wide array of attachés to Europe, Great Britain, and their North American colonies. They played important roles in the new social networks that conducted the revivals often termed the Great Awakening. They also engaged in special outreach to slaves, founding the first African church in the Western hemisphere (in the mid-1730s, on the island of St. Thomas). They erected white churches farther north in America—Savannah, Georgia (1735); Bethlehem, Pennsylvania (1741); Salem, North Carolina (1753); and elsewhere—under the leadership of Zinzendorf's assistant, Augustus Spangenberg. These churches, moreover, served as launch pads for missions to the Native American Indians, which were guided by the likes of the Moravian David Zeisberger.

Not even the Moravians, however, did missions on the scale of their descendants in the transatlantic evangelical movement. The revivals they encouraged caught fire in several regions in the late

1730s, igniting Europe's churches, bringing Protestants together in the work of the gospel, adding tens of thousands of converts to their membership rolls, and giving rise to what we now call the modern missions movement—a largely evangelical venture that eventually outstripped Catholic missions in size and scope. Like the Moravians before them, these revitalized Protestants looked for ways to cooperate in ministry with others from diverse church backgrounds (at least part of the time). And positioned as they were, a bit closer to the dissolution of European Christendom, they found more freedom than their predecessors had to forge new coalitions of "true" Christians compelled to take the faith once delivered to the ends of the earth. They also furthered a transition in evangelistic strategy begun intermittently by early Protestant leaders: a change from doing missions in a confessionalizing mode to evangelism geared toward authentic transformation—and a universal faith—that transcends all confessional and national allegiances.

The leading theologian of the evangelical movement was New England's Jonathan Edwards. A prolific Christian writer, Edwards helped countless Calvinists to back world missions—and what was known at the time as "indiscriminate evangelism"—in spite of their belief in a limited atonement. His *Freedom of the Will* (1754) taught that everyone has freedom (when not constrained physically) to do what she wills— even repent and convert—regardless of whether she is chosen for salvation (and thus will want to convert). He promoted a "concert of prayer" for "the revival of religion and the advancement of Christ's kingdom." His congregation helped to found a large mission for Indians in Stockbridge, Massachusetts. And in 1751, Edwards moved there himself, becoming the leading missionary in the colonies.[8]

---

8. Jonathan Edwards, *Freedom of the Will*, ed. Paul Ramsey, in *The Works of Jonathan Edwards*, vol. 1 (New Haven: Yale University Press, 1957), available at the Jonathan Edwards Center at Yale University, http://edwards.yale.edu/archive; Edwards, *An Humble Attempt to Promote Explicit Agreement and Visible Union of God's People in Extraordinary Prayer for the Revival of Religion and the Advancement of Christ's Kingdom on Earth, Pursuant to Scripture-Promises and Prophecies concerning the Last Time*, in Jonathan Edwards, *Apocalyptic Writings*, ed. Stephen J. Stein, *The Works of*

Edwards's *Freedom of the Will* and his *Life of David Brainerd* (1749), a profile of a passionate but short-lived American missionary who became a patron saint of the Protestant missions movement, raised missionary consciousness in Britain through the second half of the eighteenth century. Scores of Protestant Dissenters, many serving in Northamptonshire—where Edwards's ideas had excited such leaders as Philip Doddridge, John Ryland, Andrew Fuller, and William Carey—now championed the cause of international exertion. But the Calvinistic Baptists—Fuller and Carey, in particular—led the charge on the front lines of cross-cultural ministry. In 1792, Carey published a little book that soon became the most influential missions tract in history, *An Enquiry into the Obligations of Christians to Use Means for the Conversion of the Heathens.*[9] Would-be Anglophone evangelists now had their own banner, one that emphasized—with help from Edwards's treatise on the will—the *obligation* of disciples to cross cultural boundaries. Later in 1792, Carey, Fuller, and several others launched the most important missions organization of the day: the Baptist Missionary Society. Carey sailed to India in 1793, serving first in Calcutta. Others followed in his wake. And by the early nineteenth century Great Britain's evangelicals had organized a host of other, similar institutions for international ministry: the Methodist Missionary Society (1786), the London Missionary Society (1795), the Church Missionary Society (1799), the British and Foreign Bible Society (1804), the London Society for Promoting Christianity amongst the Jews (1808), and numerous other bodies.

Though the English erected the early international agencies, Americans sent the most missionaries abroad. At first, they aimed their efforts at evangelizing and educating Indians and settlers on their

---

Jonathan Edwards (New Haven: Yale University Press, 1977), 5:307–436, available at the Jonathan Edwards Center at Yale University, http://edwards.yale.edu/archive.

9. William Carey, *An Enquiry into the Obligations of Christians to Use Means for the Conversion of the Heathens* . . . (Leicester, UK: Ann Ireland, 1792), available at the Center for Study of the Life and Work of William Carey, D.D. (1761–1834), https://www.wmcarey.edu/carey/enquiry/enquiry.html.

western frontier with assistance from northeastern parachurch groups (inspired, again, by Edwards): the Connecticut Missionary Society (1797–98), the Massachusetts Missionary Society (1799), and the American Home Missionary Society (1826). But then a group of college boys expanded their horizons and stimulated action by Americans overseas. In August 1806, Samuel Mills invited several fellow Williams College students for prayer in Sloan's meadow, not far from their campus in rural Williamstown, Massachusetts. A revival at the school had aroused concern for missions, and the young men sought to pray for ministry in Asia. Caught outdoors in a thunderstorm, they hid under a haystack and committed themselves to serve the Lord in foreign lands. Soon thereafter, this event was dubbed the "Haystack Prayer Meeting."

These men prayed further for the progress of the gospel. Two years later they established the Society of the Brethren (1808), the first foreign missions organization in the country. "We can do it if we will" was their missionary motto, a principle derived from Edwards's doctrine of the will. All their members planned to serve the Lord in cross-cultural ministry. And three of them—Samuel Mills, Gordon Hall, and James Richards—continued to prepare themselves for missionary service at the recently inaugurated Andover Seminary (1808), the nation's first graduate-level theological school. They raised support for their cause, attracting other young people who became famous missionaries: Samuel Newell, Samuel Nott Jr., and the intrepid Baptist minister to Burma, Adoniram Judson. This earned the school its moniker, "the missionary seminary."

In 1810, Judson, Newell, Nott, and Hall presented themselves for foreign service before the General Association of Massachusetts (Congregationalist). The following day they helped to found their country's first "sending agency" for international missions, called the American Board of Commissioners for Foreign Missions (ABCFM). In 1812, the American Board sent Judson, Nott, Newell, Hall, and Luther Rice, along with their wives, to found a mission near Calcutta.

And by the end of the 1810s, the Board had also made deep inroads into Ceylon (Sri Lanka), the Sandwich Islands (Hawaii), Palestine, and Native America.

Among the many American missionaries whose stories bear repeating, two stand out as evangelistic trailblazers. Adoniram Judson is the most obvious of the two. Many have reckoned him his country's foremost foreign missionary. After a celebratory sendoff from the seaport in Salem (on February 19, 1812), he spent four months at sea surveying the Scripture doctrine of baptism. He disembarked at Calcutta on the seventeenth of June, continued his study of the Bible, and, before the summer's end, had rejected his denomination's practice of infant baptism. He resigned his new commission with the ABCFM (a pedobaptist organization) and was (re)baptized by immersion at Carey's mission in Serampore (north of Calcutta). He left for Burma the following year, won the support of American Baptists, and devoted the rest of his life to Burmese ministry (in today's Myanmar). He drafted a Burmese Bible and developed a Burmese dictionary. He was incarcerated and tortured during the Anglo-Burmese War. Upon his release, he worked to end the War by serving as a translator and assisting the British government with the Treaty of Yandabo (1826). He could not have accomplished as much without his three gifted wives—Ann ("Nancy") Hasseltine Judson, Sarah Hall Boardman Judson, and, nearly thirty years his junior, Emily Chubbock Judson—all important missionaries in their own right. He outlived the first two. But in April 1850, he finally succumbed to a respiratory debility. He died at sea after his doctor prescribed fresh air and a healthier clime. Sailors buried him in the depths of the Indian Ocean.

The second pioneer missionary who merits special attention lacks the celebrity of a Carey or a Judson. He died at thirty-five, just eight years after he helped to establish the ABCFM in Massachusetts. But Samuel Mills played a greater role than any early American in raising support for missions. And his service on behalf of several leading ministry groups helped to catalyze the age of Christian expansion.

Mills was born to a minister in Torringford, Connecticut. He converted during his teens in a revival (1801). He went to New England's best schools. And after providing spiritual leadership and promoting foreign ministry at Williams, Andover Seminary, and the ABCFM, he earned a license to preach (1812) and ordination (1815) among the Congregationalists. He worked first in home missions, distributing Bibles and preaching in the South and Midwest and among the poor of New York City. In 1816, he taught at the School for Educating Colored Men in nearby Parsippany, New Jersey. He also assisted in the formation of both the American Bible Society (1816) and the United Foreign Missionary Society of the Presbyterian and Dutch Reformed Churches (1816). The following year he went to West Africa, where he purchased land on behalf of the American Colonization Society (1817), an organization established to resettle freed slaves. It helped to colonize Liberia (1822) with thousands of former slaves, to remunerate their owners, and to evangelize the region. Mills died a tragic early death at sea while traveling home from Africa. His body is buried at the bottom of the Atlantic.

Former slaves are rarely mentioned in standard histories of Christian missions. But colonization played a major role in Western foreign missions, and freed slaves played a major role in African colonization. The segregationism inherent in this missionary method has disappointed many. Some of the enslaved would have preferred citizenship in the countries that enslaved them. But colonization provided many black Christian leaders with the means to shape the spiritual life of Africa. Daniel Coker, for example, became one of the first Americans to shape Sierra Leone, an English colony in West Africa that, like its neighbor Liberia, was founded (1787) as a home for former slaves. Following in the footsteps of black Baptists such as David George, who established the First African Baptist Church in Freetown, Coker led the Methodists and entered local politics. Named Isaac Wright at birth, Coker escaped slavery in Maryland and eventually helped to found the African Methodist Episcopal Church. In 1820, he sailed to

Africa as a Methodist missionary under the auspices of the American Colonization Society. Within months he was leading Sierra Leone's colonial government. He spent the rest of his life there as a leader in church and state, preparing a way for famous successors such as the ex-slave and Anglican Bishop Samuel Adjai Crowther. Lott Carey, a former slave, businessman, and lay physician, left Richmond, Virginia, in 1821 to found the first Baptist church in Liberia, the Providence Baptist Church of Monrovia (1822). By the time he died in 1828, he also served as Liberia's acting governor. Black Pietists participated in colonial missions too, even before the rise of the colonization movement in West Africa. Several of them sailed from St. Thomas in the Caribbean to Pennsylvania and Germany in the 1740s, joining native-born Africans and white Europeans in multiethnic, missions-minded Moravian communities. Black members of these groups, such as the Lutheran Frederik Svane and Moravian Christian Protten, pioneered in Christian mission on the Gold Coast of Africa (present-day Ghana). Protten, for example, served as a missionary, linguist, and teacher intermittently from 1737 until his death in 1769, joined eventually by his gifted wife, Rebecca Freundlich Protten, who died in Accra in 1780.

By the late nineteenth century, more women than men were involved in world missions. And by the early twentieth century, literally millions of women supported missionary societies, many of which were also led by females (until men took them over in the decades to come). The most celebrated woman working on a foreign field was the American Lottie Moon (born Charlotte Diggs Moon). Born in Albemarle County, Virginia, she went to Virginia Female Seminary and Albemarle Female Institute. In 1872, she left for China as a missionary, one of the first single women sent abroad by Southern Baptists. She worked for forty years in China, teaching children and evangelizing hundreds of Chinese women—both in Tengchow and Pingtu. In scores of letters and articles she published in the press, she challenged women to form their own female missionary societies and follow her in lives of foreign service. She stayed single to the end and struggled frequently with loneliness. She endured tumultuous times in her beloved land of China. Most famously, she survived the anti-Western Boxer Uprising (1899–1900), which involved a number of fierce attacks on foreign missionaries. By December 1912, her chronic illnesses and regular bouts of depression overtook her. Her friends determined to send her home, securing her passage on a ship. But like so many early missionaries, Lottie died at sea—on Christmas Eve, while docked in the harbor of Kobe, Japan.

During the early twentieth century, no one did more to promote the cause of missions than the Methodist John R. Mott. In July 1886, while studying at Cornell, Mott spent a month at Dwight L. Moody's summer Bible conference in Mount Hermon, Massachusetts. The leading revivalist in America at the end of the nineteenth century, Moody sponsored conferences in cities across the West for the study of the Bible and encouragement in missions. At Mount Hermon, with ninety-nine others, Mott subscribed to a now-famous pledge: "It is my purpose, if God permit, to become a foreign missionary." He and the "Mount Hermon Hundred" left the meeting charged for missions, persuaded their friends to sign the pledge, and thus inaugurated what they named in 1888 the Student Volunteer Movement (SVM), chaired for thirty-two years by Mott. A. T. Pierson, another leading missionary spokesman, coined its slogan or "watchword": "the evangelization of the world in this generation." The SVM failed to accomplish this ambitious goal. But during the next generation, it enlisted over twenty thousand students for missionary service.

Nothing symbolized the heyday of the Western missions movement like the 1910 World Missionary Conference in Edinburgh, Scotland. Chaired by John R. Mott, it was centered on the watchword of the SVM and convened in the Assembly Hall of the United Free Church (next to New College, Edinburgh). Planned for more than three years, it included over thirteen hundred delegates sent by leading Protestant denominations in Europe and North America. Reports were delivered and declarations made. Lord Balfour of Burleigh presided over the gathering. Spirits burned bright at the prospect of Christianizing every tribe and language. Attendees returned home more energized than ever for cooperating in mission. Their collaboration, in fact, helped to nurture the twentieth-century ecumenical movement, as several leading founders of the World Council of Churches later testified.

By the early twentieth century, the modern missions movement had clearly changed the face of the world. In 1500, there were 75,890,000 Christians in the world, comprising 18 percent of the global population. In 1600, this number stood at 100,440,000, but still represented the same percentage of the whole. By 1900, however, the church had burgeoned in extent. It was seven times larger than in 1500, and its 558,130,000 adherents comprised 35 percent of the global population. In the nineteenth century alone, it had increased from 204,980,000 to 558,130,000, or from 23 to 35 percent of the whole. The modern missionary movement left a massive global footprint. The twentieth century failed to become a "Christian century," at least in the West, where the prospect had been heralded. Two world wars, massive population growth, the decline of Christian commitment in many parts of Europe, and the increase of Islam in Asia and Africa, especially, meant that Christianity decreased by more than 2 percent of the global population over the course of the twentieth century—from roughly 35 percent to roughly 32 percent (while Islam grew from 12.6 to 22.4 percent). In the north, Christianity fell from 82 percent of the general population to 41 percent, a precipitous decline. Nonetheless, in the south, where most missions had been aimed, Christianity grew apace and, in several different places, grew like never before in history. In the majority world, the church grew from 98,670,000 in 1900 (18 percent of the general population) to 1,167,710,000 in 2000 (59 percent of the whole)—making the twentieth century in many spots a Christian century indeed. By the dawn of the third millennium, Western Christian power had contributed, ironically and all-too-often shamefully, to the vast spiritual power of the Christian global south.[10]

But the Church Has Always Been Global

Again, however, the presence of Christianity in what we call the global south is not a new phenomenon. One might be forgiven for assuming that it is, for even the most learned scholars often give such an impression. Even Justo González, a Cuban-American intellectual and one of the most globally minded thinkers of our time, has told the story of Christian doctrine as if its international scope was a late-modern invention. His best-selling, three-volume *History of Christian Thought*, used by tens of thousands of students during the past half century, is organized much like the older histories of doctrine penned by European writers—with a global component tacked on to its end. "There has been a great expansion in the scope of theology" in the twentieth century, he writes at the end of volume 3, which may "prove to be the most significant development" in the Christian thought of the last several decades. "Theology is no longer a North Atlantic enterprise. The so-called younger churches of Asia, Africa, and Latin America are making significant contributions to it."[11] This has long been the case, though, in Asia and Africa, many of whose churches date back to the first century. Though our theological forebears did not know as much as we can now learn quickly about the doctrines of far-flung Christian communions—technological advances have facilitated remarkable improvements in such knowledge—the best theologians have always done their work in conversation with Christians in other parts of the world. And Asian and African church officials have often stood among the world's best theologians. The size and shape of Christendom has

10. Statistics taken from Todd M. Johnson, "Church Growth through the Centuries," in *Encyclopedia of Christianity in the Global South*, ed. Mark A. Lamport, 2 vols. (Lanham, MD: Rowman & Littlefield, 2018), 1:169.

11. Justo L. González, *A History of Christian Thought*, vol. 3, *From the Protestant Reformation to the Twentieth Century* (Nashville: Abingdon, 1975), 390.

changed through the centuries. In the late Middle Ages, it appeared European. But the church began in Asia and spread soon to Africa long before it sank deep roots in northern Europe. It waned outside the West with the waxing of Islam. But remnants survived in the global south for centuries, preparing the ground for the resurgence of the faith in the majority world today. Our histories of doctrine should reflect these realities.

The Lord Jesus himself, of course, lived and worked in Asia, and the faith spread from Palestine to other parts of Asia very quickly after his death, resurrection, and ascension. His apostle Thomas made it to the Malabar Coast of southern India in the mid-first century. The apostle Paul evangelized much of Asia Minor (central and western Turkey) and western parts of Syria at about the same time. Believers in Adiabene (northern Iraq) received their first Christian bishop in the early second century. The first Christian kingdom (Osroene) was based in Edessa (southeastern Turkey) by the late second century. Christians could be found as far east as the empire of the Kaishans in the late second century (northeastern Afghanistan, Tajikistan, Uzbekistan, and western Pakistan). There were more than twenty bishops serving Mesopotamia in the early third century (southeastern Turkey, eastern Syria, and most of Iraq and Kuwait). King Tiridates III decreed that Christianity was the official faith of Armenia in the early fourth century. Christians lived in Georgia by the mid-fourth century. Christianity made inroads into the Himyar kingdom in the late fourth century (the southern highlands of Yemen). The first Christian Arab queen, Mawiyya, gained control of the western Tanakh in the Arabian desert after the death of her husband in the late fourth century. Christians built a monastery in Awal (Bahrain) in the late fourth century. Nestorian (or Dyophysite) Christianity gained a foothold there in the early fifth century. Nestorian Christian migrants made it all the way to China by the late sixth century. They achieved some success with the Chinese nobility in the early seventh century. Scholars translated the Bible into Syriac, Armenian, Georgian, and other Asian tongues during the first several centuries of church history. And the first seven, so-called ecumenical councils were all held in Asia. Clearly, the Christian faith has deep roots in the world's largest continent.

It also has deep roots on the continent of Africa, a few of whose churches have persisted unbroken for almost two thousand years. The Lord himself lived briefly in Egypt as a baby. Simon of Cyrene (Libya) would later carry his cross to Golgotha. Devout Jews from "Egypt and the parts of Libya belonging to Cyrene" heard the apostle Peter preach at the first Pentecost (Acts 2:10). Philip the evangelist baptized a court official of Candace, Queen of the Ethiopians, in the eighth chapter of Acts. The identity and travels of the Gospel writer Mark remain contested and mysterious, but many put him in Egypt sometime in the 40s. Others say that Mark hailed originally from Libya. Some date the existence of a church in Alexandria to the late 40s and 50s. Libyans claim that Mark planted a church in Cyrenaica (the eastern coastal region of Libya) in 66–68. He was martyred in Alexandria not long after that. The church was thriving in Egypt by the mid-second century. Clement of Alexandria began his work in Egypt in the late second century. Tertullian commenced his writing ministry in Carthage (Tunisia) in the late second century. Several believers from Madaura (Algeria) and Scillium (Tunisia) were martyred in the late second century. Pope Victor I, the first African pontiff (from the Roman province of Africa, probably from Libya) served as bishop of Rome at the end of the second century. Origen led the catechetical school of Alexandria in the early third century. Cyprian became the bishop of Carthage, his hometown, in the mid-third century. Monasticism emerged in the Egyptian countryside in the late third century. Frumentius converted King Ezana II of Aksum around 324 (Eritrea and northern Ethiopia). Frumentius later served as bishop of Aksum and helped to establish the Ethiopian Orthodox Church. The Coptic churches of Egypt and Ethiopia were founded in the mid-fifth century. Monophysite views spread throughout Nobatia (Sudan) in the mid-sixth century. Many Nubians converted to Chalcedonian Christianity at about the same time. So by the mid-sixth century there were three Christian kingdoms to be found south of Egypt: Nobatia, Makuria, and Alwa (Sudan). Many early church fathers lived, worked, or died in Africa (Clement, Tertullian, Cyprian, Athanasius, Augustine, et al.). Much of the fourth-century trinitarian controversy took place in Africa. The most influential parts of the fifth-century row over Pelagianism took place in Africa. Africa, like Asia, was a major early center of the worldwide Christian church.

The fate of Christianity in Asia and Africa, however, changed quickly in the early seventh century. The prophet Muhammad moved from Mecca to Medina in 622, gained a very large following, raised an army, and conquered most of modern Saudi Arabia. He died in Medina in 632, but his troops spread swiftly through the Middle East and Africa. They conquered Jerusalem in 637. They destroyed Alexandria in 642. And they overran most of the rest of North Africa by the mid-seventh century. Christian strongholds in Egypt and Nubia would survive for many years to come. But by the mid-eighth century, more than half the world's Christians lived in Muslim territory. Muslims now controlled many ancient Christian cities: Alexandria, Antioch, Carthage, Jerusalem, and other major centers of early Christian civilization. They colonized the hometowns of leading church fathers (such as Origen, Cyprian, Athanasius, and Augustine). Some churches persisted through the onslaughts of Islam, holding a torch for Christian faith that illuminated the paths trod by modern Christian missionaries (the Eastern Orthodox and Coptic Churches of Alexandria and the Orthodox Tewahedos of Ethiopia and Eritrea). But Islamization in many parts of Asia and Africa bore massive implications for the shape of Christianity in centuries to come.

In Asia, the birthplace of Christianity, Islam made advances during the so-called Middle Ages that continue to obstruct Christian witness on the continent. Most famously, the Seljuk Turks defeated the Byzantines in 1071 at the battle of Manzikert (in today's eastern Turkey), which soon became a stepping stone to all of Asia Minor.

On the eve of this battle, the bulk of modern Turkey identified as Christian; by the sixteenth century, it was 90 percent Muslim. The Ottomans defeated the ancient city of Constantinople in 1453, facilitating the spread of Islam into Europe. Muslim migrants had also settled much of northern India and Southeast Asia by the late Middle Ages. Consequently, the continent on which Christ was born soon became the least Christian continent on the globe. Faith in Jesus is surging now in East and Southeast Asia, with sizable Christian networks in China, Korea, Singapore, India, Malaysia, and Indonesia. Pentecostals and independents have made the greatest strides. But of the nearly fifty nations that now constitute Asia, only one, the Philippines, is predominantly Christian (it is mostly Roman Catholic).

The situation in Africa today is rather different, as many of its countries are predominantly Christian. But the Christian churches waned on that continent as well during the centuries succeeding the expansion of Islam. By 1076, Pope Gregory VII said the last remaining Roman Catholic bishop in Africa was Cyriacus of Carthage—and even his see would disappear a century later. During the late thirteenth and early fourteenth centuries, the Orthodox of Egypt and Sudan were Islamized. Ethiopia saw a rise in Christian faith in the middle years of the fourteenth century (with support from armed forces). The Portuguese colonized Atlantic and other regions of Africa beginning in the mid-fifteenth century, evangelizing in places like the Gold Coast and Congo. There were always Christian vestiges in northeastern Africa. But Muslims controlled most of the northern half of Africa before the rise of modern Christian missions.

The Promise and the Peril of Postcolonial Christian Teaching

As has now become clear, the church was far more European during the late Middle Ages and Reformation era than at any time in history, and the modern missions movement that emerged to redress this international imbalance made the global church more Western than at any time in history. By the end of the nineteenth century, there were nearly five thousand foreign missionaries serving from the United States alone. Needless to say, moreover, they packed more than the gospel and the Bible in the bags with which they sailed overseas. Western culture suffused their presentations of the faith, at least much of the time. And Western military and economic force too often guaranteed that those they went to serve would bear the weight of all their baggage. As a host of history writers has made clear in recent years, modern missionaries have often been perceived—sometimes justly—as promoters of European culture and Western expansion.

This is not the whole story, as historians of modern Western empires concede. Many missionaries repudiated imperialistic methods, as did many local Christians who contextualized their faith more fully than any foreign missionary ever could. As Andrew Porter points out with respect to British missions, many evangelists maintained spiritual motivation in their work overseas and proved ambivalent, at best, about the engines of their empire. "The growing scale of Britain's worldwide presence," he explains of the eighteenth, nineteenth, and early twentieth centuries, "made it impossible for missionaries to escape all involvement either with empire or with other facets of Britain's expansion abroad. However, that involvement was both patchy and discontinuous. . . . Attitudes ranged from total indifference or harsh criticism of empire, through discomfort and toleration, to enthusiastic support."[12]

Still, the net cultural effect of the modern missions movement, especially during the period of decolonization, was to leave many Christians in the two-thirds world seeking ways to save the baby of authentic Christian faith while discarding the bathwater of Western cultural chauvinism. From the 1940s through the 1970s, dozens of nations gained independence from Europe—from Lebanon (1943), Vietnam (1945), Jordan (1946), and India (1947) to Ghana (1957),

---

12. Andrew Porter, *Religion versus Empire? British Protestant Missionaries and Overseas Expansion, 1700–1914* (Manchester, UK: Manchester University Press, 2004), 323–24.

Nigeria (1960), Kenya (1963), and Angola (1975)—many of which included massive Christian populations. Their independence movements often featured painful struggles—many of which continue—to indigenize the practice, profession, and transmission of the Christian faith taught by colonial missionaries. In fact, the most significant development in the history of Christian doctrine in the last hundred years is the effort of these postcolonial Christians to appropriate the faith for themselves.

In Asia, where the English, Dutch, Portuguese, French, Spanish, and US Americans colonized millions, the effort to indigenize has taken many forms. In China, communist critics of Western cultural imperialists have pestered Christian converts with nationalistic slogans such as "one more Christian, one less Chinese," so Christians have worked hard to show that faith in Jesus Christ can be expressed in accordance with traditional, communal Chinese customs and culture. In India, where the higher castes benefited most from the British occupation, believers from the lower, Dalit castes have led the way in applying Christian principles in dealing with the poor and so-called untouchables. In Japan, where Christian faith still attracts less than 1 percent of the nation as a whole, indigenization has happened as believers have reflected on the suffering of Christ and the marginalization of Christians for the sake of the gospel. All over the continent, disciples have explored the ways their faith represents and fulfills native cultural aspirations long shaped by the practices of Daoism, Hinduism, Buddhism, and other Eastern religions. And evangelicals, especially, have returned to the Bible to repristinate a precolonial faith untainted by association with European history and culture—recapitulating tendencies, ironically, learned from largely ahistorical, anti-Catholic missionaries.

In Africa, where the French, British, Portuguese, Germans, and Italians recolonized most of the continent (encroaching, in some cases, on land claimed by Arabs), but where French and British forces left the largest cultural legacies, indigenization occurred at the regional, national, and continental levels as local ethnic groups rejected racist, Western stereotypes of "savage" black Africans and took control of churches and educational institutions. In Francophone Africa, the *négritude* movement paved a way for these changes. While graduate students in Paris in the 1930s, the Senegalese poet Léopold Sédar Senghor, the French Guianese poet Léon Gontran Damas, and the Martiniquais poet Aimé Césaire catalyzed black pride amid colonial repression and championed the goals of self-reliance and self-determination for black Africans. Church leaders responded with an emphasis on the African roots of global Christianity, God's love for black Christians all around the world, and the need to contextualize the faith in relation to local languages and cultures. In Anglophone Africa, indigenization continued as liturgies, doctrines, and Christian social customs were expressed in relation to traditional black mores. Leaders like the Nigerian evangelical Byang Kato, the Kenyan Anglican John Samuel Mbiti, and the Ghanaian Presbyterian Kwame Bediako mediated Christian faith amid African realities.[13] They emphasized the polycentric nature of Christianity and pointed out that most regional centers of the faith had lain well beyond Europe for the bulk of church history.

In South America, the Spanish and the Portuguese had colonized most of the continent by the mid-sixteenth century, and Napoleon's invasion of the Iberian Peninsula sparked decolonization in the early nineteenth century—much sooner than in Asia or Africa. Chile claimed independence from Spain in 1810, Argentina in 1816, Peru in 1821. Brazil declared independence from Portugal on September 7, 1822. By the time of independence, most of these countries were thoroughly Roman Catholic. But because they had no ancient Christian roots to recover, they indigenized by seeking forms of social liberation from oppressive hierarchies in both church and state, emphasizing God's concern for the poor and underprivileged, and combining

---

13. Each one did so in his own way, of course, often disagreeing with one another over the best ways to contextualize the faith in relation to African mores and cultures.

their Catholicism with folk religious practices. (The European-looking members of Latin American countries had the most wealth and power. They often marginalized mestizos and indigenous folk lower on the sociocultural ladder.) These efforts later culminated in liberation theology, a quasi-Marxist movement of the mid-twentieth century that called for social justice and political assistance to the poor and oppressed, and in several forms of Protestant and Catholic evangelicalism, most of which promoted what they called a full gospel of salvation from both personal and social sin and evil. (These movements took shape under the influence of different kinds of Western missionaries.) These theological trends, in turn, helped to shape the region's postcolonial theory and practice. Among Catholics, the Peruvian priest Gustavo Gutiérrez and Brazilian theologian Leonardo Boff offered intellectual leadership. Among evangelicals, the Ecuadorian missiologist C. René Padilla and Peruvian evangelist J. Samuel Escobar pioneered the concept of *misión integral*, calling Christians in their countries—and all around the world—to express the good news about the saving work of Christ in both spiritual and economic terms. By the 1970s, their voices had reached to the ends of the earth and informed indigenization across the global south.

Throughout the most sensitive churches of the two-thirds world, then, ministers have struggled to help people understand that one can be a faithful Christian and a card-carrying member of one's own ethnic group. And this has led to revisions in the churches' teaching ministries, revisions that now affect Christians everywhere. In the main, faithful churches in the global south today focus less on inventing new doctrines for themselves than on redressing the balance of the doctrines they promote and adapting the cultural forms and styles used to promote them. They place a much stronger emphasis on self-giving neighbor love, justice for the poor, and Spirit-filled witness in their worship and outreach than most other Christians, especially other Christians who descend from the more privileged churches of Eastern Orthodoxy and Western Christendom. At times, though, the effort to appropriate the faith has led to radical departures from the faith once delivered, most often under the influence of liberal intellectuals from Europe and North America (an irony often lost on the people in the pews). In the name of contextualizing Christian faith authentically, unshackling it from structures of oppression and injustice, and expressing it in terms of their own cultural preferences, postcolonial prophets sometimes cut their people off from the rest of God's family, belittling cardinal doctrines of historic Christianity—on sin, repentance, the atoning work of Christ, the nature of the church, and other crucial matters—as opiates of the people, or Western forms of piety that tie them to their former colonizers. In the words of those gathered at the inaugural convention of the Ecumenical Association of Third World Theologians (EATWOT), held in Dar es Salaam in August 1976, a forthright departure from the teachings of the West is required to make room for new, majority world voices: "The theologies from Europe and North America are dominant today in our churches and represent one form of cultural domination. . . . We must, in order to be faithful to the Gospel and to our peoples, reflect on the realities of our own situations and interpret the Word of God in relation to these realities. . . . We are prepared for a radical break in epistemology which makes commitment the first act of theology and engages in critical reflection on praxis of the reality of the Third World."[14] Less globally minded thinkers put the matter more starkly.

As I hope is now clear, though, the church does not need modern methods of liberation derived from the West to contextualize the Christian faith for all of God's people. The church has always been global, so decolonization and unity in Christ across ethnic, racial, and sociocultural lines can proceed hand in hand. This is easier said than done. It requires careful thinking, altruistic love, and serious self-sacrifice by everyone involved, especially those in the West. Still, Christians need to live more fully into the truths of the gospel and

---

14. "Statement of the Ecumenical Dialogue of Third World Theologians," *Occasional Bulletin of Missionary Research* 1, no. 1 (January 1977): 20.

history regarding our polycentric—and Christocentric—spiritual constitution, recovering from centuries of historical amnesia pertaining to our multiethnic, international makeup, resisting the canard that we are only now global, in order to render our teaching more authentic, comprehensive, and contextual again.

Teaching the Christian Faith across Both Time and Space

What I mean by this is that Christians need to help each other teach the Christian faith across both time and space. In chapter 1, I emphasized the teaching of the faith in continuity with the past (teaching across time). Now, here in chapter 2, I am stressing the importance of listening to believers in other parts of the world and accounting for their understanding of Christian faith and practice as we inculcate doctrine in our own backyards (teaching across space). Both disciplines are ways of catechizing God's family in and with—indeed under—what we name in the Niceno-Constantinopolitan Creed the "one, holy, catholic, and apostolic church." Catechesis across space is a method of paying heed to the ethnic diversity within the Christian church, allowing for the indigenization of doctrine in a multitude of languages and cultures, while honoring the unity of God's global family. After all the careful listening to faraway Christians that ought to be a part of the teaching of God's people, orthodox Christians will affirm one faith. And though our teachers should account for the hearing and the doing of the Word by brothers and sisters in other parts of the world, at the end of the day they all stand fast on the Bible and profess "one Lord, one faith, one baptism, one God and Father of all, who is above all and through all and in all" (Eph. 4:5–6).

The Scottish scholar Andrew Walls is especially helpful here. In a spate of publications on cross-cultural ministry, he offers sage advice about teaching across space. Christianity has always been an incarnational faith, he says, stressing the importance of contextual teaching and learning. "No one ever meets universal Christianity in itself; we only ever meet Christianity in a local form, and that means a historically, culturally conditioned form." We "need not fear this," he adds. "When God became man, he became historically, culturally conditioned man, in a particular time and place. What he became, we need not fear to be. There is nothing wrong with having local forms of Christianity—provided that we remember that they *are* local." Neither do we need to fear cross-cultural contact or assume that global cultures stand as timeless, changeless forms that are tainted or degraded by exchanges with outsiders. Interference can enrich us. Cultural change is not all bad. The concern of faithful teachers should be simply to oppose all cultural aggression and imperial chauvinism, unilateral cultural force exerted with ethnocentric prejudice. As Walls concludes the matter, "the principal dangers of" cultural contact "come when one party insists that its own local features have universal validity."[15]

The challenge for cross-cultural Christian teaching, says Walls, is to balance what he calls the faith's "indigenizing principle" with its twin, the "pilgrim principle." Inasmuch as these principles have shaped the way that many now teach across space, they deserve attention here. The indigenizing principle, for Walls, reminds us that Christianity is always and only articulated in concrete cultural forms: "The fact . . . that 'if any man is in Christ he is a new creation' [II Corinthians 5:17] does not mean that he starts or continues his life in a vacuum, or that his mind is a blank table. It has been formed by his own culture and history, and since God has accepted him as he is, his Christian mind will continue to be influenced by what was in it before. And this is as true for groups as for persons. All churches are culture churches—including our own."[16]

15. Andrew F. Walls, "The American Dimension in the History of the Missionary Movement," in *Earthen Vessels: American Evangelicals and Foreign Missions, 1880–1980*, ed. Joel A. Carpenter and Wilbert R. Shenk (Grand Rapids: Eerdmans, 1990), 19, 24.

16. Andrew F. Walls, "The Gospel as Prisoner and Liberator of Culture," in *The Missionary Movement in Christian History: Studies in the Transmission of Faith* (Maryknoll, NY: Orbis Books, 1996), 9.

The pilgrim principle, by contrast, says that all Christianity is universal too. Christians are pilgrims and strangers here. We have no abiding, earthly city (Heb. 11:10, 13–16, 39–40). We and our cultures need to be transformed by the heavenly King of kings. Walls unpacks this principle with profound historical wisdom:

> The Christian is given an adoptive past. He is linked to the people of God in all generations (like him, members of the faith family), and most strangely of all, to the whole history of Israel, the curious continuity of the race of the faithful Abraham. By this means, the history of Israel is part of Church history, and all Christians of whatever nationality, are landed by adoption with several millennia of someone else's history, with a whole set of ideas, concepts, and assumptions which do not necessarily square with the rest of their cultural inheritance; and the Church in every land, of whatever race and type of society, has this same adoptive past by which it needs to interpret the fundamentals of the faith. The adoption into Israel becomes a "universalizing" factor, bringing Christians of all cultures and ages together through a common inheritance, lest any of us make the Christian faith such a place to feel at home that no one else can live there; and bringing into everyone's society some sort of outside reference.[17]

The question of our identity, our place, within the church, then, needs to be engaged by all Christian people everywhere in reference to both our differences and unity as pilgrims, siblings in God's family, fellow heirs of God with Christ (Rom. 8:14–17).

Here again, however, this is easier said than done. Take the case of Christian faith in modern China, for example. Chinese Christians have a host of good reasons to resist the call to honor and appropriate the pilgrim principle—to suspect it as a ruse, a Trojan horse put forward to overwhelm their differences and assimilate their churches to a Eurocentric faith. Such suspicion, furthermore, sorely complicates

17. Walls, "The Gospel as Prisoner and Liberator of Culture," 9.

the task set before us in this chapter. It is difficult, yea daunting, to define Christian identity in a context of concern regarding the history of Christian missions, in a time and place where many are uneasy about appearing too dependent on, or rooted in, those sectors of the pilgrim throng tethered to the West.

Christianity is growing as quickly in parts of mainland China as it has ever grown, anywhere, before. And over the course of recent decades, this growth has been indigenous—far less dependent on the churches of the West than Western churches are dependent on their ancient, Asian forebears. Chinese missionaries today are taking risks in untold numbers for the sake of Jesus Christ, spreading their own faith abroad and playing a major role in the history of the global missions movement. As historian Daniel Bays noted a generation ago, "On any given Sunday there are almost certainly more Protestants in church in China than in all of Europe."[18] This is even truer today. Nevertheless, many patriots complain that the Christian faith is "foreign," or Western, insufficiently Chinese. "One more Christian, one less Chinese," goes the slogan. All too many deem the Christian faith a form of Western culture.

In their efforts to contextualize the faith, moreover, many Chinese Christians have sought to cut the cords sometimes said to bind them to the West, to the history of its churches and their doctrinal concerns. Kevin Yao has shown that this began a century ago, when local leaders took control of their own congregations and distanced them from Western denominations:

> As Chinese Christian communities grew stronger and more indepen-
> dent in the early twentieth century, Chinese Christians started to take
> leadership roles in the life of churches. For them Western denomina-
> tionalism was irrelevant and even absurd in the Chinese setting and
> harmful to the progress of Christianity in China. . . . Liberal church
> leaders and intellectuals viewed denominationalism as the obstacle

18. Daniel H. Bays, "Chinese Protestant Christianity Today," *China Quarterly*, no. 174 (June 2003): 488.

to indigenizing Christianity in China. . . . On the other hand, many conservative and evangelical church leaders viewed denominations as an unbiblical invention.[19]

Philip Leung, among others, adds that many Chinese have also scorned their own history, which has been written all too often from a Western point of view. Though a "China-centered" history has emerged in recent years,[20] the habit of leaving most history behind has helped Christians to discard the heavy baggage often brought by the missionaries. It has enabled them to develop a uniquely Chinese faith—and to base that faith more squarely on the Bible.

This rather ahistorical manner of contextualizing the faith, this habit of leaving most history behind as we appropriate its doctrine, is not unique to China. Many Christians around the world, particularly those tied to the evangelical movements, share a tendency to teach without much reference to church history. In the name of indigenization (catechism across space) they have all too often neglected to convey those aspects of the Christian tradition not connected very closely, or directly, to their own (catechism across time). But ironically, and sadly, this ahistorical style of teaching Christians who they are often perpetuates a typically Western evangelical problem: the age-old habit of holding hard-won doctrines loosely, standing only on the Bible, repackaging the faith in the name of local relevance, and ignoring the rest of the church. Not only does this habit undermine the global nature of the holy catholic church. It makes the Christian faith difficult to render in any but presentist and ethnocentric terms.

The task that faces those who want to honor and appropriate the international legacy of all local Christians—and teach across space—is to contextualize the faith without becoming more parochial, less cath-

19. Kevin Xiyi Yao, The Fundamentalist Movement among Protestant Missionaries in China, 1920–1937 (Lanham, MD: University Press of America, 2003), 185.

20. Philip Yuen-Sang Leung, "Mission History versus Church History: The Case of China Historiography," in Enlarging the Story: Perspectives on Writing World Christian History, ed. Wilbert R. Shenk (Maryknoll, NY: Orbis Books, 2002), 54–74.

olic, in the process. We need to teach with the whole church—in every time and place. We need to shed the common assumption that our faith is mostly Western. And we need to be more honest about the sins of the past that keep us from living and working together as the body of Christ in the world.

God has used Christian missions to spread the gospel around the world. He has done so, moreover, in a variety of ways, all culturally conditioned and historically particular, and many beset with much ahistorical ignorance. Some ambassadors of Christ have proved more ethnocentric than others. But all of them have shared their faith in idiomatic terms, in contemporaneous forms. Only recently, moreover, have we come to see with clarity—and embrace with sensitivity—what Philip Leung has called "a multi-centered view of the church,"[21] a view in which the faith has no single, earthly center, but is polycentric in nature. As Zhang Kaiyuan reminds us,

> Christianity does not belong to any particular nation or nationality. The process of Christianity's spread worldwide is also the process of its transplantation into one new culture after another. Meanwhile, for many centuries the dream of converting non-Christian areas actually involved the indigenization of Christianity in these areas. Of course, normal cultural communication is a two-way interactive process. From the perspective of us historians, the universality of Christianity lies in its theological core, and is formed through multilingual and multicultural interpretation, development, and gradual integration.[22]

Perhaps majority world Christians will lead the way in demonstrating how to contextualize the faith without domesticating it—how to render it their own without repeating the sins of the past and universalizing their social and cultural preferences.

21. Leung, "Mission History versus Church History," 74.

22. Zhang Kaiyuan, "Chinese Perspective—a Brief Review of the Historical Research on Christianity in China," in *China and Christianity: Burdened Past, Hopeful Future*, ed. Stephen Uhalley Jr. and Xiaoxin Wu (Armonk, NY: M. E. Sharpe, 2001), 29.

3

Doctrine as Church Teaching
for the Shaping of Faith and Practice

But as for you, continue in what you have learned and firmly believed, knowing from whom you learned it, and how from childhood you have known the sacred writings that are able to instruct you for salvation through faith in Christ Jesus. All scripture is inspired by God and is useful for teaching, for reproof, for correction, and for training in righteousness, so that everyone who belongs to God may be proficient, equipped for every good work.

—2 Timothy 3:14–17

By this point on our journey through the history of the issues that attend the task of teaching Christian faith with understanding, fidelity, and wisdom, one might think that we would have passed all the key construction zones and seen most of the road signs erected by church leaders eager to help us on our way. We have crossed the roughest stretches of debate about the Spirit's role in leading us "into all the truth" (John 14–16). We learned that the Christian church has always been global and that its most helpful guides teach across time and space. We have struggled with the challenge of transmitting one faith (Eph. 4), teaching the faith once delivered (Jude) in a unified manner while accounting for diversity in God's global family. We have yet to look directly, though, at several basic questions whose answers keep the very best instructors on task with intelligence and prudence: Just what is Christian doctrine? How is it devised? Should it ever be revised? How so? By whom? And why does any of this matter? I dealt obliquely with a few of these questions in chapter 1, which reviewed some of the history lying behind their varied answers. But here, in chapter 3, I engage them more directly and systematically, paying due attention to modern theories of doctrine, "so that everyone who belongs to God may be proficient, equipped for every good work" (2 Tim. 3).

What Is Christian Doctrine?

The first of these questions sounds simpler than it is. For not only do its commentators often disagree about the subject matter taught in the name of Christian doctrine, the primary audience to whom it is addressed, and the ideal setting for instruction of this sort. They even disagree about the meaning of the word "doctrine" itself.

The English word "doctrine" comes from the Latin word *doctrina*, meaning "teaching, instruction, education, or learning." Etymologically, then, doctrine means "teaching or learning." In the Greek New Testament, there are two key nouns for doctrine, *didaskalia* (διδα-σκαλία) and *didachē* (διδαχή), both of which are kin to the Greek verb *didaskō* (διδάσκω). *Didaskalia* is employed far more frequently than *didachē*. Both nouns appear in texts like Titus 1:9, "he [an elder] must have a firm grasp of the word that is trustworthy in accordance with the teaching [διδαχήν], so that he may be able both to preach with sound doctrine [διδασκαλίᾳ] and to refute those who contradict it." There are minor variations in the way these terms are used. But they both refer mostly to the kerygmatic message of the Lord and his apostles and the ethical requirements of faithful

Christian disciples. Further, both are synonymous with the Greek word *dogma* (δόγμα), which means "doctrine, ordinance, precept, or decree" and appears in Scripture texts such as Acts 16:4: "As they [Paul, Silas, and Timothy] went from town to town, they delivered to them for observance the decisions [δόγματα] that had been reached by the apostles and elders who were in Jerusalem." In the ancient world, *dogma* meant "that which was deemed right and good by authorities and promulgated accordingly." Its semantic range was narrower than those of our other two Greek words for doctrine. In early church history, *didaskalia* and *didachē* meant "any teaching useful for advancement in discipleship" while *dogma* referred, at least much of the time, to "decisions meant to rule faith and practice."

Ever since that time, Christian leaders have negotiated the things we ought to teach in the name of Christian doctrine, whether and when Christian doctrines should function as rules of faith, and how best to teach doctrine to others. This has led to somewhat inconsistent uses of the term, in which the meanings of the three New Testament words for doctrine—and assumptions about the nature of theological education—are combined and weighted variously by teachers engaged in different doctrinal tasks. Some have majored in sophisticated theological discourse on the best ways to formulate the precepts taught. Others have systematized such high-level discourse for use in teaching doctrine in academic contexts. A few have taken their own churches' doctrines for granted and created pedagogies for delivering those teachings at the congregational level.

The history reviewed in chapter 1 of this book further complicates the task of defining Christian doctrine in a unitary way. Premodern church leaders disagreed about the ways in which God's Spirit leads us into truth and helps us as we represent divine truth to others. Western Christians prioritized the inculcation of Scripture and tradition as distilled by duly authorized teachers (disagreeing somewhat about the people who qualified as authorized teachers). In the East, a stricter emphasis was placed on the writings of the early church fathers and statements of the first seven ecumenical councils. Theology, moreover, the Orthodox have said, is a way of knowing God by helping Christians walk the "three ways" to unity with him—the way of catharsis/purification, the way of illumination, and that of perfection/ deification—in which information plays a less important role than practice and persistence over time through the mysteries of faith. During the sixteenth century, Protestants revised their received understandings of the content and sources of authority of doctrine. By the eighteenth century, both Protestants and Catholics faced far more critics of their teaching than ever before, many of whom castigated any and all traditionary, top-down teaching of the faith to the people. And in the nineteenth century, the modern academic disciplines of religion and theology congealed in universities, colleges, and seminaries. They were promulgated in contexts now largely disconnected from the churches and their leaders, where historicism, scientism, higher biblical criticism, and naturalistic views of world history were trending and the project of passing on a "faith once to delivered" to the saints by the Lord and divinely sanctioned messengers seemed hopelessly naïve.

The fact that the body of Christ has always been global, as seen in chapter 2, raises even more challenges for those who want to represent the nature of its doctrine in a unified manner. In some times and places, intellectual understanding of the tenets of the faith has been the number one goal in transmitting Christian doctrine—and teachers have diverged from one another over the tenets. In other international contexts, the ethical dimensions of the faith have been preeminent—and teachers have diverged over the ethics espoused. Some have demonstrated far more passion than others for defending rules and boundaries of the church's faith and practice. And believers in the global south have sometimes resisted the embrace of Christian precepts codified in Europe. John Mbiti spoke for many when he wrote of African Christians,

There is little or no particular interest among African Christians to engage in credal formulations of faith. They want to live and not just to recite their faith. It is a living faith, a faith for the whole body: head, stomach, reproductive system, feet and hands; and the whole spirit, since in African views of the world, body and spirit are an entity, separable only at death. . . . Instead of reciting creeds—and many Christians do exactly that, following the tradition from some churches of the West—African Christians are more at home in dancing their faith, in celebrating their faith, in shouting their faith (through jubilation), singing their faith, being possessed by the Holy Spirit of their faith and demonstrating the frontiers of their faith. Traditional Christian creeds have their place in African Christianity, but people are not content only to recite their faith in the form of creeds. They want to demonstrate that their faith is not only in the head but in the whole person—body and spirit—and that it works, when it bears children, when it leads to martyrdom and when it drives out unwanted spiritual forces. In these forms it flows in the blood.[1]

More African Christians have composed creeds and confessions than Mbiti understood back in 1986. Nonetheless, his point is apt. God's family has many ways of handing on the faith.

These historical realities complexify the study of Christian doctrine today, at least for those who work responsibly and ecumenically. Since the late nineteenth century, though, a steady stream of scholars has attempted to chart a modern way forward for such learners, some of them with marvelous erudition and practicality. Several in this stream shape the current conversation concerning doctrine, its nature, purposes, and functions. And the first of these thinkers to merit special attention is Adolf von Harnack, whose *Lehrbuch der Dogmengeschichte* (*The History of Dogma*, 1886–89) still informs leading doctors of the church.

Harnack managed our complexities by pruning them. He sought to shear the Christian faith of most of its traditions, authorities,

---

1. John S. Mbiti, *Bible and Theology in African Christianity* (Nairobi: Oxford University Press, 1986), 127.

cultural packaging, and metaphysical teaching, leaving only what he deemed to be its timeless moral lessons on the fatherhood of God, the brotherhood of humans, and the infinite importance of every human soul. He contended for the recovery of Christianity's "essence" (*Wesen* in German), the kernel of the faith, which he often described as the presence of God in the world, personified in Jesus and seen in his love for humanity and struggle to realize the reign of God on earth. Harnack urged church teachers to forgo all else, to discard the faith's "husk" as they transmit its "kernel."[2] He conflated doctrine and dogma and deprecated both as corruptions of the pure word of Jesus in the Gospels. "Dogma in its conception and development," he stressed, "is a work of the Greek spirit on the soil of the Gospel." Under the influence of ancient Greek philosophy, that is, many early theologians took the essence of Christianity and turned it into a creed, a metaphysical system, imposing it on others with assistance from an ever-more-bureaucratic church. As Martin Luther and his kin came to see in later years, though, the kernel of their faith was too potent for containment by a single cultural system or philosophical husk. Over and over again in history, it has broken through the time-bound accretions it accumulated and offered up its quiddity in pristine power. And this was just what Harnack hoped would happen in his own day. He sought a pure and simple Christian faith that animated others with the ethics of the kingdom.[3]

Many of Harnack's successors have found his history of dogma—and conflation of dogma and doctrine—distasteful. Most have labored as professors, nearly always in the academy, sometimes in the church, for whom Harnack's "kernel" offered too little nourishment to Chris-

2. The locus classicus of this teaching is Adolf von Harnack, *Das Wesen des Christentums: Sechzehn Vorlesungen vor Studierenden aller Facultäten im Wintersemester 1899/1900 an der Universität Berlin gehalten* (Leipzig: J. C. Hinrichs, 1900); trans. Thomas Bailey Saunders as *What Is Christianity?* (1957; repr., Philadelphia: Fortress, 1986).

3. Adolf von Harnack, *Lehrbuch der Dogmengeschichte, Vierte neu durchgearbeitete und vermehrte Auflage*, 3 vols. (Freiburg im Breisgau: J. C. B. Mohr, 1909–10); English quotation from Adolph Harnack, *History of Dogma*, 3rd ed., trans. Neil Buchanan, 7 vols. in 4 (New York: Dover, 1961), 1:17.

tian disciples and appeared to be a product of his own liberal Lutheranism, which stood in need of the pruner's shears itself. The most important of these commentators was Jaroslav Pelikan, whose five-volume masterwork, *The Christian Tradition* (1971–89), served partly as a rejoinder to Harnack's *History of Dogma*. As Pelikan pronounced on the very first page of *The Christian Tradition*, Christian doctrine, at its best, is not an alien imposition on the church by its leaders. It is rather "what the church of Jesus Christ believes, teaches, and confesses on the basis of the word of God." Doctrine "is the business of the church," that is. It derives from devotion to divine revelation in Christian faith and practice and, in turn, shapes Christian faith and practice in the church. Its history "is not to be equated with the history of theology," Pelikan averred in stark opposition to Harnack. "If it is, the historian runs the danger of exaggerating the significance of the idiosyncratic thought of individual theologians at the expense of the common faith of the church."[4] Or as he clarified this elsewhere,

> To find a substitute for Harnack's definition of the history of doctrine as history of dogma, it is necessary to define doctrine in a manner that is simultaneously more comprehensive and more restrictive: more comprehensive in that the polemical and juridical expressions of doctrine in the form of dogmatic decrees and promulgations are not isolated from other expressions of doctrine, such as preaching, instruction, exegesis, liturgy, and spirituality; more restrictive in that the range and content of the doctrines considered are not determined in the first place by the quarrels among theologians but by the development of those doctrines themselves.[5]

4. Jaroslav Pelikan, *The Christian Tradition: A History of the Development of Doctrine*, vol. 1, *The Emergence of the Catholic Tradition (100–600)* (Chicago: University of Chicago Press, 1971), 1, 3.

5. Jaroslav Pelikan, *Historical Theology: Continuity and Change in Christian Doctrine*, Theological Resources (London: Hutchinson, 1971), 95. He said much the same in a variety of places, having offered a more fulsome definition of Christian doctrine in *Development of Christian Doctrine: Some Historical Prolegomena* (New Haven: Yale University Press, 1969), 143: "Christian doctrine is what the Church believes, teaches, and confesses as it prays and suffers, serves and obeys, celebrates and awaits the coming of the kingdom of God."

For Pelikan, doctrine was a form of Christian practice, not a philosophical exercise owned by academics. Much like Mbiti, albeit in a rather more Western cultural mode, he contended that doctrine is a "whole person" affair.[6]

The most important person to write about the character of doctrine after Pelikan's opus was his friend and Yale colleague George Lindbeck. An ecumenical theologian with a personal investment in Lutheran-Catholic dialogue, Lindbeck managed the complexities we face by treating doctrines as regulations meant to shape faith and practice, not truth claims formulable in only one way. In *The Nature of Doctrine* (1984), a monograph that captivated a generation of theorists, he contended for a "cultural-linguistic" view of doctrine as distinguished primarily from two chief rivals: a "cognitive-propositional" approach to Christian doctrine (in which doctrines serve as "truth claims about objective realities," as they have for most of history) and an "experiential-expressive" conceptualization of doctrine (in which doctrines function as "noninformative and nondiscursive symbols of inner feelings, attitudes, or existential orientations," as they have in many modern and liberal forms of religion). On the latter two views, Lindbeck suggested, "It is difficult to envision the possibility of doctrinal reconciliation without capitulation," a paramount concern for this postliberal ecumenist. Either one group's truth claim is right and others wrong (cognitive-propositionalism) or doctrinal terminology is not meant to outlast or symbolize more than its root sensibilities and needs no cross-cultural reconciliation (experiential-expressivism).[7]

Lindbeck's cultural-linguistic view of doctrine, by contrast, permits mediation across Christian time and space. For "rules, unlike propositions or expressive symbols, retain an invariant meaning under changing conditions of compatibility and conflict. For example," he explained, "the rules 'Drive on the left' and 'Drive on the right' are

---

6. Mbiti, *Bible and Theology in African Christianity*, 127.

7. George A. Lindbeck, *The Nature of Doctrine: Religion and Theology in a Postliberal Age* (Philadelphia: Westminster, 1984), 16.

unequivocal in meaning and unequivocally opposed, yet both may be binding: one in Britain and the other in the United States." Contradictions between rules "can in some instances be resolved, not by altering one or both of them, but by specifying when or where they apply, or by stipulating which of the competing directives takes precedence." Thus doctrines, for Lindbeck, *when functioning as doctrines*, will involve propositions and generate feelings, but their language serves to regulate Christian faith and practice in the context of the church; they do not make ontological, categorical claims about realities that transcend their own cultural systems. Even ancient creedal claims from major ecumenical councils "do not on the basis of rule theory have doctrinal authority," he noted controversially. "That authority belongs rather to the rules they instantiate," rules about the need for all Christians everywhere to safeguard "monotheism . . . and Christological maximalism." Decrees that descend from Nicaea and Chalcedon "represent historically conditioned formulations of doctrines that are unconditionally and permanently necessary to mainstream Christian identity. Rule theory," for Lindbeck, applying this theory to his own church's most basic creedal formulations, means "giving these creeds the status that the major Christian traditions have attributed to them, but with the understanding that they are permanently authoritative paradigms, not formulas to be slavishly repeated."[8]

To many of his critics, Lindbeck's cultural-linguistic approach to Christian doctrine verged on relativism, especially with respect to truth claims.[9] Scores of leading theologians have expressed this concern, but none quite as potently as Alister McGrath, an Oxford professor and Northern Irish Anglican priest. In *The Genesis of Doctrine: A Study*

---

8. Lindbeck, *The Nature of Doctrine*, 18–19, 74, 96.
9. It should be pointed out here that, in numerous discussions of his postliberal theory of the nature of doctrine, Lindbeck denied that he was advocating relativism, insisting instead that the spiritual realities to which faith points and in which Christians trust, while affirmed within intrasystemic conditions, nonetheless exist objectively. Christian affirmations, that is, correspond to independent, objective realities. Start with George A. Lindbeck, "George Lindbeck Replies to Avery Cardinal Dulles," *First Things* 139 (January 2004): 13–15, a response to Avery Cardinal Dulles, "Postmodern Ecumenism," *First Things* 136 (October 2003): 57–61.

in the Foundations of Doctrinal Criticism (1990), McGrath contended that Lindbeck's interpretation of doctrine misconstrued the history of doctrine and reduced both the nature and functions of doctrine to a misleading and far-too-theoretical caricature. "I would suggest," wrote McGrath, "that there is at best a partial overlap between what Lindbeck describes as 'doctrine,' and the historical phenomenon of doctrine." Lindbeck's reduction "does not coincide . . . with the complex agglomerate of social, cognitive and existential parameters implicated in a fully nuanced account of doctrine as an historical phenomenon." McGrath did not undertake his own theory of doctrine but rather sought to describe it in its fullness and complexity, stressing that especially "cognitive and experiential approaches to doctrine" have "more to commend them than Lindbeck suggests." McGrath highlighted "four major dimensions" of doctrine: (1) its role in social demarcation; (2) its source in and interpretation of "the Christian narrative"; (3) its rendering of experience; and (4) the truth claims it makes. He emphasized that none of these dimensions should be isolated and turned into a comprehensive theory of the whole. And he explained that the age-old ministry of handing on divine truth through doctrine continues to thrive today.[10]

The last of our late-modern experts on doctrine to merit special attention is Kevin J. Vanhoozer, an American theologian who has taught in the University of Edinburgh, Wheaton College, and Trinity Evangelical Divinity School. In *The Drama of Doctrine: A Canonical-Linguistic Approach to Christian Theology* (2005), whose title is a play on Lindbeck's doctrinal theory, Vanhoozer made use of dramaturgical philosophy to move past the notion that our doctrines are just facts that require affirmation and to spotlight the role of Christian doctrine in directing our performance of the drama of redemption as scripted in the Bible. "The cultural-linguistic turn characteristic of postliberal and other types of postmodern theology," he wrote, "is a

10. Alister E. McGrath, *The Genesis of Doctrine: A Study in the Foundations of Doctrinal Criticism* (Grand Rapids: Eerdmans, 1997; orig. 1990), 34, 37.

salient reminder that theology exists to serve the life of the church. Yet the turn to church practice seems to have come," he continued, "at the expense of biblical authority." Vanhoozer's theory of doctrine, a product of his evangelical Protestant commitments, echoed Lindbeck's judgment that "meaning and truth are crucially related to language use." But it parted ways with Lindbeck by insisting that "the normative use" of language in the church "is ultimately not that of ecclesial *culture* but of the biblical *canon*." Vanhoozer suggested that we "participate rightly" in the drama of redemption only if we understand "what the drama is all about." He said we gain this knowledge in the text of holy Scripture and that the church's art "is to 'render' the meaning of the drama of redemption in new sociohistorical contexts through its corporate life." The drama of doctrine, for Vanhoozer, featured Christian performance of the language of the Bible, prompted and directed by the canon's main themes and improvised when needed in response to situations not covered by the script, to the end of wise, loving Christian practice in the world.[11]

This thumbnail sketch of the most consequential late-modern work on the subject is enough to make clear that even definitions of doctrine come with serious implications for the ways in which we represent the Christian faith to others. Harnack favored rather minimal synopses of what he insisted was the essence of the faith. Lindbeck allowed for more detailed pedagogies—the sort often used in Roman Catholic and Lutheran churches—but also called for pluralism and mutual forbearance across theological cultures. Their opponents usually wanted more fulsome definitions of their own churches' teachings. But we all continue to struggle with how best to bequeath our confessional traditions to the people in our care without ignoring or dishonoring the legacies of others in the global family of God.

Careful readers may have noticed that the best-known experts on the definition of doctrine in the modern age are Protestants. This

---

11. Kevin J. Vanhoozer, *The Drama of Doctrine: A Canonical-Linguistic Approach to Christian Theology* (Louisville: Westminster John Knox, 2005), 16, 77–78, 184.

is not to deny that many Orthodox and Roman Catholic scholars have addressed it, often with great erudition,[12] some of whom are better known on topics like the sources of authority for doctrine, the development of doctrine, and the roles of the liturgy and Christian spirituality in doctrinal formation. It is only to say that Protestants have borne the greatest burden to define and transmit the faith in contexts more distant from the built-in, taken-for-granted, institutional hierarchies and magisterial practices observed by other Christians and assumed by many to define the nature of doctrine. Protestants have had more explaining to do about their own approach to representing Christian faith to others. In fact, as Protestants have quarreled over the nature and purpose of doctrine, their differences of opinion over how much catholic teaching and practice to embrace, and how best to embrace it, have informed their very definitions of doctrine.

For the sake of this project, which is written for the faithful and their teachers everywhere—and takes seriously the challenge of accounting for the doctrine of the whole people of God, past and present, near and far—I will not be adopting only one, modern theory of the nature and purpose of doctrine. That would be to restrict my presentation of its history. I will emphasize here—more simply and ecumenically than some have done before—that Christian doctrine is church teaching for the shaping of faith and practice. It derives from the teaching of our Lord Jesus Christ, his prophets, and apostles, primarily as given in the canon of Holy Scripture, but is formed

---

12. Traditional Catholic dogmatic works have often begun with definitions of theology and dogmatic teaching. See, for example, Adolphe Tanquerey, *Brevior synopsis theologiae dogmaticae*, 3rd ed. (Rome: Desclée, 1919), 1–8, available at Internet Archive, https://archive.org/details /breviorsynopsist00tanq; Joseph Pohle, *God: His Knowability, Essence, and Attributes; A Dogmatic Treatise, Prefaced by a Brief General Introduction to the Study of Dogmatic Theology*, trans. Arthur Preuss (St. Louis: B. Herder, 1911), 1–14, available at Google Books, https://books.google.com /books?id=gfQOAAAAQAAJ; Joseph Wilhelm and Thomas B. Scannell, *A Manual of Catholic Theology, Based on Scheeben's "Dogmatik,"* vol. 1, *The Sources of Theological Knowledge, God, Creation and the Supernatural Order*, 4th ed. (London: Kegan Paul, Trench, Trübner, 1909), xvii–xviii, available at Internet Archive, https://archive.org/details/manualofcatholic01scheiala.

through the history of reflection on that teaching overseen by the authorized leaders of the churches. It gives rise to and reflects upon our rules of faith and practice—and actual growth in godliness, *theosis* to some—and accounts for the experience of God in the world, but it does so in a manner that is guided by the Word of God, explained and applied by those equipped and appointed for this task by God's people.

In the pages of this project, "doctrine" is not a synonym for "Christian thought in general," "dogmatics," or "theology." "Doctrine" represents the faith and practice of the church and is taught in congregations in a manner that is guided by their creeds, confessions, and contemporary authorities. The history of this teaching involves the history of the churches' work to justify their doctrines, interpreting them with theories adapted from the intellectual cultures they inhabit. But doctrine per se is what is taught in the churches for the shaping of faith and practice. It is taught in many forms: catechisms, liturgies, prayers, hymns, and creeds, not to mention Bible studies, statements of faith, and confessions. As we saw in chapter 1, the "law of prayer" often functions as a law of belief (*lex orandi, lex credendi*). There is more than one way to teach the Christian faith to others. Deacon Ephrem the Syrian understood this rule. He taught doctrine (and fought against a wide range of heresies) through captivating poetry, most potently, though certainly not exclusively, in his fourth-century *Hymns against Heresies*. "I have been made a partaker in love by Him," he sang about the Savior in his *Hymns on the Nativity*, enchanting those who heard him with the beauty of Christology, "and I have burst into song. With pure hymns I shall sing hallelujahs to Him." More recently, the poet Frances Havergal, a faithful lay Anglican from England, showed that prayers and songs instruct. "Oh, teach me, Lord, that I may teach / the precious truths which you impart," she penned in an oft-printed nineteenth-century hymn. "And wing my words that they may reach / the hidden depths of many a heart." Pelikan was right. Christian doctrine reaches people in a variety of ways. But just how, we ask next, are its messages devised?[13]

How Is Doctrine Devised?

As we saw in chapter 1, the initial Christian efforts to proclaim and defend the deposit of the faith led to liturgies, apologies, catechisms, and creeds, which were used by church leaders to inculcate doctrine. With the canonization of Scripture, though, the rise of a fully fledged conciliar tradition, and developments in East and West that led to the Great Schism of 1054, theologians mounted ever-more-detailed arguments on the relative authority and proper relationship of Scripture, tradition, and teachers of the church in the formulation of doctrine. The question how doctrine is devised became contentious and far more difficult to answer than ever before. But despite the varied views that emerged during the late Middle Ages and modern period, a few main responses to the question coalesced and helped to clarify the differences between what became the Eastern Orthodox, Roman Catholic, and Protestant divisions of the global Christian church.

The Orthodox Church

In the Orthodox Church, the regulation of teaching is the province of the bishops, all of whom are equal in ecclesial authority and committed to the transmission of faith in accordance with the first seven ecumenical councils (convened before the ninth-century Photian debacle exacerbated tensions between Eastern and Western leaders and reduced the reach of later church councils).[14] The Bible is a

---

13. Ephrem the Syrian, *Hymns on the Nativity* [*De Nativitate*], no. 2, in *Ephrem the Syrian: Hymns*, trans. Kathleen E. McVey (New York: Paulist Press, 1989), 76, available in a different translation at New Advent, https://www.newadvent.org/fathers/3703.htm; Frances R. Havergal, "Lord, Speak to Me, That I May Speak" (1872), published in hundreds of hymnals and available at https://hymnary.org/text/lord_speak_to_me_that_i_may_speak.

14. Though I have mentioned these ecumenical councils above, a listing of them here will reinforce this chronological point about the place of the Photian controversy in undermining the reach of later councils deemed "ecumenical" by Roman Catholics: Nicaea (325); Constantinople

primal source of Orthodox doctrine—some say the chief source. But the canon of Scripture itself is a product, most Orthodox theologians contend, of decisions by the fathers and early church councils. Likewise, local church councils, church fathers and teachers, the creeds, and, to a lesser extent, occasional confessions give shape to Eastern doctrine, especially inasmuch as they have gained a broad hearing and reception in the churches. Still, the teaching of the first seven councils is normative. Their ecumenical judgments are believed in the East to be the primary means by which the Lord guides his people.

In the wake of these councils, church teaching in the East evolved mainly through the liturgy and spiritual instruction. The bishops did continue to refine Eastern doctrine, largely in response to both Protestant and Catholic confessionalization in the West (which will be explored in detail in the future volume of this project). In so doing, they appealed to the writings of the fathers and doctors of the church, interpreting the Orthodox tradition synthetically and specifying doctrine with the help of both councils and authoritative teachers of the Orthodox faith. As the Russian Orthodox theologian Georges Florovsky reminded readers frequently,

> The historical and practical methods of recognizing sacred and catholic tradition can be many; that of assembling Ecumenical Councils is but one of them, and not the only one. This does not mean that it is unnecessary to convoke councils and conferences. But it may so happen that during the council the truth will be expressed by the minority. And what is still more important, the truth may be revealed even without a council. The opinions of the Fathers and of the ecumenical Doctors of the Church frequently have greater spiritual value and finality than

---

(381); Ephesus (431); Chalcedon (451); Constantinople II (553); Constantinople III (680–81); and Nicaea II (787). The Photian schism (863–67), which involved a disagreement over the addition in the West of the *filioque* clause to the Nicene Creed, was occasioned by the opposition of Pope Nicholas I to the appointment of Photius, a layman, to the partriarchate of Constantinople by the Byzantine Emperor Michael III. None of the later councils counted "ecumenical" by Catholics (who count twenty-one ecumenical councils altogether, the eighth of which is said to be Constantinople IV, convened in 869 to combat the power of Photius) is honored as such by the Orthodox.

the definitions of certain councils. And these opinions do not need to be verified and accepted by "universal consent."[15]

The Bulgarian New Testament scholar Nikolaj Nikaronovič Glubokovský once quipped on behalf of the Orthodox, "The West incessantly asks us for the symbolical books of Orthodoxy. We have no need of them. The faith of the seven first councils is sufficient for us."[16] Such statements by themselves, though, can mislead auditors. The Orthodox maintain a venerable tradition of divine pedagogy, one informed most directly by the ecumenical councils. But they do so with help from a wealth of theologians, liturgical developments, sacred art, and devotions. Their bishops seek to transmit the Orthodox faith in a Spirit-led manner well suited to the times.

The bishopric of Rome holds a special place in the East, but not like in the West. The pope is neither supreme nor infallible in Orthodoxy. Those adjectives apply only to Scripture and, for some, to the ecumenical councils. The pope is, rather, first among equals in the East. He is recognized widely as the church's first bishop. But his primacy derives from Rome's historical importance in the rise of Christianity—and after the decline of the ancient Roman Empire the bishop, or patriarch, of Constantinople (often dubbed the New Rome) came to share the pope's status as the bishop serving nearest to the center of earthly power.[17] Papal primacy is a product of world history for Easterners. It is honored as a matter of fact, not divine right. Each bishop in the East rules his own, local church, and episcopal authority is shared among the bishops. Only those in the episcopacy teach with authority to represent doctrine that ought to be believed by the Orthodox faithful. But the teaching of the bishops

15. Georges Florovsky, *Bible, Church, Tradition: An Eastern Orthodox View*, in *The Collected Works of Georges Florovsky* (Belmont, MA: Nordland, 1972), 1:52.

16. Nikolaj Nikaronovič Glubokovský as recorded in S. Herbert Scott, *The Eastern Churches and the Papacy* (London: Sheed & Ward, 1928), 351.

17. This status was encoded in the twenty-eighth canon of the council of Chalcedon, which canon was later nullified by Rome.

both derives from and answers to the faith of the Orthodox Church as a whole.

The Roman Catholic Church

In the Roman Catholic Church, doctrine is derived from both Scripture and tradition as interpreted by members of the church's teaching office, or Roman magisterium, the bishops of the church in communion with the pope. The Bible, decrees of the ecumenical councils, the pope, and the Roman Catholic Church as a whole (as represented by the pope) are understood to be infallible, the pope not as a private man but only insofar as he defines faith and morals "from the chair" (*ex cathedra*), as the vicar of Christ on earth. None of the other bishops has the same status or authority. But all the bishops bear responsibility to serve as the church's main teachers, making sure that the faithful understand the Word of God. On the ground, this means that most priests, school teachers, and diocesan officials, under the guidance of their bishops, represent Catholic teaching from Scripture and a wide range of theological sources—ancient creeds, prayers and liturgies, catechisms, pontifical encyclicals, and more—in the context of the parish on behalf of the teaching office of the global church.

This approach to the derivation of doctrine was defined more clearly than ever before in the last two centuries, especially in the last two councils considered ecumenical by Roman Catholic leaders. At the First Vatican Council, a "dogmatic constitution" on pontifical authority was published and promoted, entitled *Pastor Aeternus* ("The Eternal Shepherd," 1870), which underscored the apostolic primacy of Peter, its continuity in and through the Roman Catholic papacy, its bearing on the practices of papal supremacy, and the doctrine of papal infallibility. "That apostolic primacy which the Roman pontiff possesses as successor of Peter, the prince of the apostles, includes also the supreme power of teaching," it proclaimed. "When the Roman pontiff speaks *ex cathedra*, that is, when, in the exercise of his office as shepherd and teacher of all Christians, in virtue of his supreme apostolic authority, he defines a doctrine concerning faith or morals to be held by the whole church, he possesses, by the divine assistance promised to him in blessed Peter, that infallibility which the divine Redeemer willed his church to enjoy in defining doctrine concerning faith or morals." Moreover, "should anyone . . . have the temerity to reject this definition of ours: let him be anathema." At the Second Vatican Council, another dogmatic constitution was released, called *Dei Verbum* ("The Word of God," 1965), which defined the right relationship of Scripture and tradition in Roman Catholic teaching. "Tradition and scripture together form a single sacred deposit of the word of God, entrusted to the church," its drafters averred. The duty of interpreting and handing on this word, "whether in its written form or in that of tradition, has been entrusted only to those charged with the church's ongoing teaching function." And "by God's wise design, tradition, scripture and the church's teaching function are so connected and associated that one does not stand without the others, but all together, and each in its own way . . . contribute effectively to the salvation of souls." In the widely published *Catechism of the Catholic Church* (1992), whose instruction on the issues stands squarely on *Dei Verbum*, Scripture and tradition are said to constitute a unified deposit of the Word of God. "The task of interpreting the Word of God authentically," it warns those who use it, "has been entrusted solely to the Magisterium of the Church, that is, to the Pope and to the bishops in communion with him." These dogmas are plainer and more powerful today than they ever were before the modern period.[18]

As we saw in chapter 1, though, Roman Catholic thinkers have long argued that their doctrine has developed incrementally, in organic fashion, as the Spirit led bishops to make explicit the tenets that had

18. First Vatican Council, session 4, July 18, 1870, in *Decrees of the Ecumenical Councils*, ed. Norman P. Tanner, 2 vols. (London: Sheed & Ward, 1990), 2:815–16; Second Vatican Council, session 8, November 18, 1965, in Tanner, *Decrees of the Ecumenical Councils*, 2:975; *Catechismus Catholicae Ecclesiae*, part 1, section 1, article 2 (trans., *Catechism of the Catholic Church, with Modification from the Editio Typica* [New York: Doubleday, 1995], 35, available at the website of the Vatican, http://www.vatican.va/archive/ENG0015/_INDEX.HTM).

often been implied in the piety and practice of the faithful through the ages. The logic of Aquinas with respect to church councils applies categorically for Catholics on the matter. "In every council of the Church a symbol of faith has been drawn up to meet some prevalent error condemned in the council at that time," Thomas expounded in his *Summa Theologiae* (1265–74). "Hence subsequent councils are not to be described as making a new symbol of faith; but what was implicitly contained in the first symbol was explained by some addition directed against rising heresies."[19] Yves Congar later confessed that modern Catholic theologians, in an effort to adjudicate rival developments and justify doctrines that were not defined before (about the papacy and Blessed Virgin Mary, for example), had elevated the role of the Roman magisterium vis-à-vis tradition, increasing its power to *define* the tradition in the present retroactively. But he also reiterated that Scripture and tradition are complete, in themselves, to deliver God's Word to the faithful in the churches (*totum in scriptura, totum in traditione*), and "tradition renders explicitly things which Scripture contains merely in principle: such things for example as the scriptural canon, the canon of the sacraments, and many points not only in Marian theology but in 'theology' in general, such as the personal divinity of the Holy Spirit or the equality of the divine Persons."[20]

Protestant Communions

In the Protestant communions, doctrine is usually said to come from Scripture alone, though commentators disagree on whether and to what extent traditions of interpretation, creeds, confessions, and church officials ought to play a role in shaping the instruction of the faithful from the Bible. Only Scripture is infallible. Traditions, popes, bishops, creeds, and councils are revisable—and sometimes opposed.

19. Thomas Aquinas, *Summa Theologiae* I, q. 36, a. 2; trans. at New Advent, https://www.newadvent.org/summa/1036.htm.

20. Yves M.-J. Congar, *The Meaning of Tradition*, trans. A. N. Woodrow, The Twentieth Century Encyclopedia of Catholicism 3 (New York: Hawthorn Books, 1964), 154–55 (orig. *La Tradition et la vie de l'Église* [Paris: Librarie Arthème Fayard, 1963]).

As Reformed Protestant leaders have repeated since the middle of the seventeenth century, their churches are "reformed and always being reformed" on the basis of the Word of God (*ecclesia reformata, semper reformanda*). Many early Protestant spokesmen called the papacy the antichrist, in part for its refusal to reform in accordance with their own views of Scripture. (During the past several decades such derision has declined and, in most Protestant contexts, virtually disappeared.) In practice, though, of course, all Protestants who seek to be catholic, or orthodox, and even some who don't, employ traditions of several kinds—interpretive, cultural, social, ecclesial—in teaching God's people.

Protestants are so diverse and decentralized that it is difficult and even misleading to describe them by quoting influential representatives. Still, in the early and most formative age of Protestant church history, no one did as much to articulate and defend an evangelical perspective on the derivation of doctrine as Martin Chemnitz, a north German Lutheran theologian. In response to the Catholic Church's censure of the Reformation *solas* at the Council of Trent (1545–63)—salvation is by grace alone (*sola gratia*), apprehended by faith alone (*sola fide*), as taught by Scripture alone (*sola scriptura*)— Chemnitz championed the supremacy of Scripture in doctrinal formulation and adherence to tradition in the church's teaching ministries only insofar as tradition is consonant with Scripture. In a lengthy diatribe on the relevant decrees of the Tridentine fathers, "Concerning Traditions, From the First Decree of the Fourth Session of the Council of Trent," included in his *Examination of the Council of Trent* (1565–73), Chemnitz pleaded for precision in the contest raging over catholic traditions. "The word 'traditions' was not used by the ancients in one and the same way," he suggested, "and because the traditions of which mention is made in the writings of the ancients are not all of the same kind, the papalists sophistically mix together such testimonies without discrimination and, as the saying goes, whitewash all traditions from one pot in order that they may disguise them under the pretext and appearance of antiquity." He proceeded to distinguish eight kinds of tradition: (1) doctrine given orally by apostles that was later written down in the Scriptures; (2) testimony about the books intended by apostles for inclusion in the canon; (3) apostolic traditions that concern the rule of faith, derived from the Scriptures and wielded against heresy; (4) traditions concerning the interpretation of Scripture; (5) traditions "not set forth in so many letters and syllables in Scripture but . . . brought together from clear testimonies of Scripture by way of good, certain, firm, and clear reasoning"; (6) traditions concerning the consensus of the fathers on matters of importance; (7) traditions concerning rites and customs that are traced by some to the apostles; and (8) "traditions which pertain both to faith and morals and which cannot be proved with any testimony of Scripture but which the Synod of Trent nevertheless commands to be received and venerated with the same reverence and devotion as the Scripture itself." Chemnitz concluded by contending that the Protestants embraced most of these (or at least the Lutherans did). They affirmed those traditions with a clear basis in Scripture, allowed those traditions that do not contradict it (and are edifying to Christians), and held loosely to traditions that might (in certain circumstances) obstruct true faith and genuine piety. They only opposed those traditions that contradicted the Bible.[21]

Not *all* Protestants proved quite so catholic. The Reformed trimmed the liturgy, stripped church buildings, and pruned church teaching of everything that lacked a direct warrant in Scripture (taking a stricter, more negative approach than the Lutherans to rites and customs deemed apostolic in Rome). The radical reformers did away with most traditions for the sake of repristinating apostolic practice. And in the age of the Enlightenment, some Protestant reformers grew more liberal and doubtful about deriving doctrine—or *authoritative*

---

21. Martin Chemnitz, *Examination of the Council of Trent, Part I*, trans. Fred Kramer (St. Louis: Concordia, 1971; orig. *Examinis Concilii Tridentini*, 4 parts [Frankfurt, 1565–73]), 217–307 (quotations from 220, 249, 272–73).

doctrine—from the Scriptures themselves. (Many Catholics did too, especially later on, but Protestants pioneered the practices of biblical and doctrinal criticism in much greater numbers before the mid-twentieth century, "liberating" Christians to be their own teachers.) Europeans staffed the vanguard of this liberating trend, but after World War II, increasing numbers of Americans in mainline churches made emblematic statements on its import for teaching Christian faith in congregations. Presbyterian Ed Farley pointed out that even though most believers still behaved as though "the house of authority" for teaching Christian doctrine remained operational—with its "classical" criteria for formulating truth, like the canon of the Bible and authoritative traditions regarding its significance for Christian profession—it had fallen quite flat, like a flimsy house of cards.[22] Congregationalist David Kelsey said that even the concepts of Scripture, the canon, and authority for Christians proved far less stable than usually met the eye. "'Scripture,' he contended, "is not something objective that different theologians simply use differently. In actual practice it is concretely construed in irreducibly different ways." There is "certainly no one 'standard' or 'normative' meaning of 'authority,'" he added. In practice, Christian pedagogues mean many different things by "biblical authority." Churches should acknowledge this, Kelsey suggested, and release their people from the confines of reductive, oppressive, and tribal Christian faith.[23]

Despite these modern trends, most Protestants have maintained a robust commitment to the role of church teaching in shaping faith and practice. As many now repeat, they are "always being reformed" on the basis of the Word. Their doctrines are revisable, never set in stone. In the face of modern challenges to Scripture and tradition, though, their evangelical members have invested more in doctrine

22. See especially Edward Farley, *Ecclesial Reflection: An Anatomy of Theological Method* (Philadelphia: Fortress, 1982); quotations from 165–68.

23. David H. Kelsey, *Proving Doctrine: The Uses of Scripture in Modern Theology* (Harrisburg, PA: Trinity Press International, 1999), 1–2.

than at any time since the seventeenth century. The English Anglican theologian John Webster has functioned as a spokesman for many. "Creeds and confessional formulae," wrote Webster, "properly emerge out of one of the primary and defining activities of the church, the *act of confession*. In that act, which is constantly to characterize the life of the church, the church binds itself to the gospel. Confession is the act of astonished, fearful and grateful acknowledgement that the gospel is the one word by which to live and die; in making its confession, the church lifts up its voice to do what it *must* do—speak with amazement of the goodness and truth of the gospel and the gospel's God."[24] Such confession must never cease, Webster averred. The conviction it expresses "cannot simply be thought of as capital in the bank. Confession is a permanently occurring event; the church never reaches a point where the act of obedient confession can be put behind it as something which *has been* made, and which can be replaced by a text which will become the icon of the church as a confessing community."[25] Rather, confessional materials, Webster summarized, wielding language long commonplace in Protestant church history, "have the authority of a norm which is itself normed; they have real yet conditional, limited and subordinate authority to bind the church; they are a penultimate but not an ultimate word."[26]

Should Doctrine Ever Be Revised? How So? And by Whom?

This Protestant commitment—at least in theory, often in practice—to the time-bound, provisional, permutable position of all man-made teaching tools raises more questions about the practices of handing on the faith in congregations. What should be our attitude toward these materials (creeds, confessions, and other catechetical tools)?

24. John Webster, "Confession and Confessions," in *Confessing God: Essays in Christian Dogmatics II* (London: T&T Clark, 2005), 69.
25. Webster, "Confession and Confessions," 73.
26. Webster, "Confession and Confessions," 80.

Should they ever be changed? Do they regulate teaching unless and until they are revised? Do we use them because (*quia*) they epitomize the doctrinal deliverances of Scripture or only insofar as (*quatenus*) teachers find them true to the Word? Should we mandate a strict adherence to them by our leaders or only subscription to the substance of their doctrines? If our churches decide that revisions are required, how should they be made, by whom, and by what right?

Before the nineteenth century, most Christians assumed that the teaching they received in their churches was eternal. It was either a faithful summary of God's Word to them, exportable in the same form anywhere in time; a reliable extrapolation sanctioned by tradition; or a recent specification deserving of their trust because handed down by leaders with authority to represent the faith of the church. When believers disagreed about doctrinal matters, they usually disagreed about how best to maintain "the faith that was once for all entrusted to the saints" (Jude 3). During the nineteenth century, though, this began to change, especially in Protestant intellectual networks affected by the rise of historicism (but also in networks engaged with Cardinal Newman—more on this below). By the early twentieth century, a growing number of Orthodox and Roman Catholic scholars had addressed this change as well, now entertaining the notion that their teaching had developed over the course of church history, growing more thorough in response to a complex, ever-changing world.

This shift was shaped profoundly by the modern universities. By the mid-nineteenth century, church history had become a major academic discipline. The Bible and theology were taught in many schools by scholars steeped in world history and historical methodology. It was obvious to some of them that Christian teaching changed from time to time and place to place. And a growing number of churchmen involved in these schools—like Merle d'Aubigné (a Swiss Reformed scholar), Johann August Neander (a Jewish-German Lutheran), John Henry Newman (an Anglican turned Catholic), Philip Schaff (who was Swiss-German-American Reformed), George Park Fisher (an

American), and scores of their students—tried to demonstrate, though not without extensive resistance, that churches and their teachers could remain orthodox while acknowledging adjustments in their teaching over time. (Less faithful academics employed historical methodology to undermine the pedagogical work of the clergy, provoking suspicion of these methods in the churches.)

By the mid-twentieth century, Roman Catholics and even a few Orthodox thinkers had imported this thinking into monasteries and churches. Some pioneered movements that would later be referred to as the *nouvelle théologie* ("new theology," a title its proponents tried to keep at arm's length but that meant historical criticism of static, scholastic, abstracted understandings of the teaching of the church), *ressourcement* (a "return to the sources" for purchase on the present), and "neo-patristic" thought (a term more common in the East)—all of which demonstrated doctrinal responsiveness and recontextualization of the faith over time and played a major role in shaping both the ecumenical movement and the Second Vatican Council. Divines like the French Cardinals Henri de Lubac, Yves Congar, and Jean Daniélou; the German Jesuit priest and theologian Karl Rahner; and the Swiss priest and theologian Hans Urs von Balthasar encouraged Roman Catholics to think developmentally about their tradition. And while priest-theologians like the Russian Georges Florovsky and Romanian Dumitru Stăniloae usually bypassed the *language* of development in Orthodox circles, they appealed to church fathers and spiritual exemplars to oppose what they labeled Western, abstract dogma (or scholastic and largely ahistorical catechesis) in the Orthodox churches. Some of these thinkers had progressive views of history. Others clearly did not. But all of them denied that church teaching should be static. Some of them denied that church teaching is always the same (*semper eadem*). Each in his own way affirmed that the best teaching lives and breathes in Christ by the power of the Spirit, facilitates progressive sanctification in believers (called *theosis* in the East), and responds well to ever-new challenges to faith.

The Orthodox Church

In the Orthodox Church, most leaders have eschewed the words "change" and "development" in catechetical contexts. Some say that the Orthodox reject the very notion that their teaching has developed. Even major Eastern scholars such Georges Florovsky, Andrew Louth, and Vladimir Lossky have expressed unease around suggestions that their doctrine has evolved over time, or unfolded organically, or that Christian teaching now surpasses that of the fathers. Louth has written firmly against the logic of development, implying that the Orthodox agree to oppose it. "If development means that there is an historical advance in Christian doctrine," he contends, "making our understanding of the faith deeper or more profound than that of the Fathers, ... then such a notion of development cannot be accepted as a category of Orthodox theology."[27]

Some Orthodox thinkers, though, have said things that sound like what Catholics and orthodox Protestants have meant by their affirmations of doctrinal development. Lossky, for instance, has suggested that "'dogmatic tradition' ... can be increased by receiving, to the extent that may be necessary, new expressions of revealed Truth, formulated by the Church."[28] Florovsky, supporting the work of Vladimir Soloviev (a Russian intellectual of the late nineteenth century), explained that, for Soloviev, "'dogmatic development' consists of the fact that the original 'pledge of faith,' while remaining totally inviolate and unaltered, is increasingly disclosed and clarified for the human consciousness."[29] The British Orthodox thinker John Behr has underscored that often good teachers give us "more detailed and

27. Andrew Louth, "Is Development of Doctrine a Valid Category for Orthodox Theology?," in *Orthodoxy and Western Culture: A Collection of Essays Honoring Jaroslav Pelikan on His Eightieth Birthday*, ed. Valerie Hotchkiss and Patrick Henry (Crestwood, NY: St. Vladimir's Seminary Press, 2005), 55.

28. Vladimir Lossky, *In the Image and Likeness of God* (Crestwood, NY: St. Vladimir's Seminary Press, 2001), 166.

29. Georges Florovsky, *Ways of Russian Theology: Part Two*, in Florovsky's *Collected Works* (Vaduz, Liechtenstein: Büchervertriebsanstalt, 1987), 6:158.

comprehensive explanations elaborated in defense of one and the same faith."[30] The Ukrainian-American Paul Gavrilyuk has argued that even "the principle of the unchangeability of the Nicene faith did not preclude doctrinal development; on the contrary," he writes, "this principle provided a robust metaphysical foundation for doctrinal development. If the Orthodox leadership had not come to the agreement over the Nicene faith, the debate over the foundations" of Orthodox tradition "would have encumbered . . . later doctrinal developments, especially in the area of Christology and doctrine of God."[31] And the American Orthodox theologian Daniel Lattier has worked to bring the Eastern churches into a constructive conversation with Cardinal Newman, contending that the idea of doctrinal development as represented by Newman "is in fundamental harmony with the Orthodox understanding of Tradition."[32]

The Orthodox agree that revelation does not change. The deposit of the faith was given once and for all. They disagree, though, about whether (and to what extent) the church's understanding of revelation can improve: leaders such as Lossky and Louth say no; Florovsky, Stăniloae, Behr, Gavrilyuk, and Lattier say yes. Indeed, Stăniloae states that "it is not only the mission of [new doctrinal expressions] to be

---

30. John Behr, "Scripture, the Gospel, and Orthodoxy," *St. Vladimir's Theological Quarterly* 43 (1999): 248.

31. Paul L. Gavrilyuk, "The Legacy of the Council of Nicaea in the Orthodox Tradition: The Principle of Unchangeability and the Hermeneutic of Continuity," in *The Cambridge Companion to the Council of Nicaea*, ed. Young Richard Kim (Cambridge: Cambridge University Press, 2021), 333.

32. Daniel J. Lattier, "The Orthodox Rejection of Doctrinal Development," *Pro Ecclesia* 20 (Fall 2011): 409; Lattier, "John Henry Newman and Georges Florovsky: An Orthodox-Catholic Dialogue on the Development of Doctrine" (PhD diss., Duquesne University, 2012). There are more liberal, usually Western, Eastern Orthodox thinkers, often converts to Orthodoxy, who echo liberal Protestants when dealing with this matter. Most famously, David Bentley Hart has denounced "the illusion that a doctrinal symbol provides anything like a perspicuous . . . grasp of the truth it indicates." Doctrinal formulations, for Hart, "are not really explanations of anything, so much as constraints upon certain forms of thought or (more accurately) language. It is not really obvious that they are the sort of statements that one would even know how to believe in a 'propositional' or 'literal' way, given that they seem designed as much to preserve the right sort of ignorance as to convey 'correct' information." Such lay academics, though—even those like Hart who hold out hope in a final causality or horizon that calls and clarifies the history of doctrine apocalyptically—do not represent the teaching of the Orthodox churches. See David Bentley Hart, *Tradition and Apocalypse: An Essay on the Future of Christian Belief* (Grand Rapids: Baker Academic, 2022), 159.

the means which by their novelty will awaken the human mind to see anew the amazing meaning and importance of the words and formulas of Scripture and Tradition. It is not only a question of an exterior renewal, or of an 'aggiornamento' of language. It is impossible to separate language and content so clearly as that. If one uses new expressions, one throws new light onto the content expressed."[33] In assertions like this, some Orthodox leaders sanction doctrinal development on non-Western terms.

Church teaching does not evolve in the Orthodox East. Church history does not improve upon the faith that was once for all entrusted to the saints, unpacked by the fathers, and codified at the (first seven) ecumenical councils. But the church's understanding and transmission of this heritage, some Orthodox confess, has developed over time for the good of God's people. This does not render Christian doctrine better in the present than it was long ago. But it does render doctrine more thorough and likely to meet the questions and challenges that modern people face. Christian catechists should foster an adherence to tradition, especially as handed down by church fathers and councils. But the bishops should also teach, some Orthodox advise, in a language informed by the history of the church after 787 (when the last of the ancient church councils was convened). Insofar as such pedagogy is guided by the bishops and engenders growth in godliness, many understand it as a means by which the Spirit of God leads us into truth—and they implement it in local congregations.

The Roman Catholic Church

In the Roman Catholic Church, things have changed more dramatically, especially over the course of the last several decades. Before Vatican II, most Catholics still repudiated the notion of development. During Vatican II, Newman's theory gained ground among many of the bishops, fanned the spirit of *aggiornamento* wafting through the

---

33. Dumitru Stăniloae, "The Orthodox Conception of Tradition and the Development of Doctrine," *Sobornost* 5 (1969): 660.

meetings ("bringing up to date," a spirit called for by Popes John XXIII and Paul VI), and undergirded the council fathers' efforts at reform. In the wake of Vatican II, Catholics often led the way in theological reflection on doctrinal development. This change was precipitated by centuries of ad hoc work by theologians. As it surfaced during the council in the mid-twentieth century, though, it rocked the Catholic Church and changed the landscape of ecumenical dialogue and catechesis all around the world.

Proponents of development in Roman Catholic teaching find its roots in the Bible and ancient church history. Bible doctrine was developed over the course of the Old and New Testaments, they note. And several early church fathers also hinted that the original deposit of the faith would be unpacked and promoted more completely over time. Even Vincent of Lérins, whose famous canon required that we teach only that which "was believed everywhere [*ubique*], always [*semper*], and by all [*ab omnibus*]," contended in the very same ancient publication that such conservatism allowed for development as well. Some will ask while pondering this canon, he predicted, "Shall there, then, be no progress in Christ's Church? Certainly," Vincent made haste to respond, "all possible progress."

> For what being is there, so envious of men, so full of hatred to God, who would seek to forbid it? Yet on condition that it be real progress [*profectus*], not alteration [*permutatio*] of the faith. For progress requires that the subject be enlarged in itself [*res amplificetur*], alteration, that it be transformed into something else [*aliquid ex alio in aliud*]. The intelligence, then, the knowledge, the wisdom, as well of individuals as of all, as well of one man as of the whole Church, ought, in the course of ages and centuries, to increase and make much and vigorous progress; but yet only in its own kind; that is to say, in the same doctrine, in the same sense, and in the same meaning.[34]

34. Vincent of Lérins, *Comonitoria* 2.23; trans. at New Advent, https://www.newadvent.org /fathers/3506.htm. Ironically, Newman himself criticized Vincent, especially for the ways in

As careful readers will have seen by now, and others will see later, this anticipated Newman's own theory of development.

In the long Middle Ages, from the fall of ancient Rome to the era of the Renaissance, Catholics rarely paid close attention to development. It did not become a locus of scholastic conversation. But some did comment on adjustments in the doctrines of the church over time. Augustine explained that, in the providence of God, heretics occasioned more precise church teaching. They "vindicated the Catholic Church," he claimed in a comment on the fifty-fifth psalm (early fifth century), by provoking more detailed biblical exposition on the part of the faithful. "For was the Trinity perfectly treated of before the Arians snarled. . . . Was repentance perfectly treated of before the Novatians opposed?" No, he replied. For as Saint Paul wrote in 1 Corinthians 11:19, "it is needful . . . that also heresies there be, in order that men proved may be made manifest among you."[35] In his *Answer to Maximinus the Arian* (427–28), moreover, a two-volume treatise published after his debate with that homoian[36] bishop, Augustine confessed that decrees of church councils sometimes contradict themselves and that Catholic formulations had not always prevailed. Still, the Scriptures provided common ground, he insisted, on which teachers of the churches can work through their differences. "By the

---

which Protestants employed him in opposition to Rome, wielding Vincent's canon against modern Catholic developments. See John Henry Newman, *An Essay on the Development of Christian Doctrine*, 6th ed., Notre Dame Series in the Great Books (Notre Dame, IN: University of Notre Dame Press, 1989), 10–27, where Newman contends, "It does not seem possible, then, to avoid the conclusion that, whatever be the proper key for harmonizing the records and documents of the early and later Church, and true as the dictum of Vincentius must be considered in the abstract, and possible as its application might be in his own age, when he might almost ask the primitive centuries for their testimony, it is hardly available now, or effective of any satisfactory result. The solution it offers is as difficult as the original problem" (27).

35. Augustine, *Expositions on Psalms* [*Enarrationes in Psalmos*], Psalm 55, 21; trans. at New Advent, https://www.newadvent.org/fathers/1801055.htm. The quotation of 1 Cor. 11:19 is from this translation of Augustine.

36. As we will see in the future volume of this project, the homoians were a network of semi-Arian thinkers who denied that the Son is consubstantial (ὁμοούσιος, *homoousios*) with the Father, as required by the fathers of the Council of Nicaea (325). They affirmed instead that God's Son is similar (ὅμοιος, *homoios*) to the Father, a doctrine that prevailed in many fourth-century churches.

authority of the scriptures that are not the property of anyone [like rival councils were], but the common witnesses for both of us, let position do battle with position, case with case, reason with reason," he challenged his antagonists.[37]

Aquinas advanced an approach to alterations in the church's teaching ministries that serves as a standard for many to this day, one appealed to even by promoters of development after Vatican II. He affirmed that those closest to the Lord Jesus Christ, "like John the Baptist" or "the apostles, had a fuller knowledge of the mysteries of faith; for even with regard to man's state," he explained in the *Summa Theologiae* (1265–74), "we find that the perfection of manhood comes in youth, and that a man's state is all the more perfect, whether before or after, the nearer it is to the time of his youth."[38] Further, apostolic knowledge of the Lord and his ways is provided in definitive form within the leaves of Scripture.[39] This is not to say, however, that such knowledge does not grow. On the contrary, it sometimes expands over time in response to new challenges and widespread confusion. "In every council of the Church," Thomas wrote in the *Summa*, "a symbol of faith has been drawn up to meet some prevalent error condemned in the council at that time. Hence subsequent councils are not to be described as making a new symbol of faith; but what was implicitly contained in the first symbol was explained by some addition directed against rising heresies."[40] Like Augustine before him, he taught that doctrine is refined in response to false teaching. And this helped him make sense of the feeling that some statements of the early church fathers had become obsolete or, better, outmoded. As he put this in

37. Augustine, *Contra maximinum haereticum Arianorum episcopum* 2.14.3; trans. from *Arianism and Other Heresies*, trans. Roland J. Teske, The Works of Saint Augustine: A Translation for the 21st Century I/18 (Hyde Park, NY: New City, 1995), 282.

38. Thomas Aquinas, *Summa Theologiae* II-II, q. 1, a. 7; trans. at New Advent, https://www.newadvent.org/summa/3001.htm.

39. Thomas Aquinas, *Scripta super libros Sententiarum* III, d. 25, q. 1, a. 1, 3; Aquinas, *Summa Theologia* II-II, q. 1, a. 9, trans. at New Advent, https://www.newadvent.org/summa/3001.htm.

40. Aquinas, *Summa Theologiae* I, q. 36, a. 2; trans. at New Advent, https://www.newadvent.org/summa/1036.htm.

his book *Against the Errors of the Greeks* (1263), "There are ... two reasons why some of the statements of the ancient Greek Fathers strike our contemporaries as dubious." The second of these reasons was largely linguistic: "because many things which sound well enough in Greek do not perhaps, sound well in Latin." The first pertained more to the development of doctrine:

> Because once errors regarding the faith arose, the holy Doctors of the Church became more circumspect in the way they expounded points of faith, so as to exclude these errors. It is clear, for example, that the Doctors who lived before the error of Arius did not speak so expressly about the unity of the divine essence as the Doctors who came afterwards. And the same happened in the case of other errors. This is quite evident not only in regard to Doctors in general, but in respect to one particularly distinguished Doctor, Augustine [a Latin church father]. For in the books he published after the rise of the Pelagian heresy he spoke more cautiously about the freedom of the human will than he had done in his books published before the rise of said heresy. In these earlier works, while defending the will against the Manichees, he made certain statements which the Pelagians, who rejected divine grace, used in support of their error. It is, therefore, no wonder if after the appearance of various errors, present day teachers of the faith speak more cautiously and more selectively so as to steer clear of any kind of heresy. Hence, if there are found some points in statements of the ancient Fathers not expressed with the caution moderns find appropriate to observe, their statements are not to be ridiculed or rejected; on the other hand neither are they to be overextended, but reverently interpreted.[41]

Popes and councils, for Aquinas, played a role in spelling out what was less clear before, but they did so while preserving the deposit of the

41. Aquinas, *Contra Errores Graecorum* (1263) I, prooemium (prologue); trans. at CalibreLibrary, https://isidore.co/aquinas/english/ContraErrGraecorum.htm#0; cf. Aquinas, *Summa Theologiae*, II-II, q. 1, a. 10.

faith. "It should be said," he repeated, "that in any council whatsoever some creed was instituted on account of some error that is condemned in the council. Hence a later council was not making another creed than the first, but that which is implicitly contained in the first creed is explained against the existing heresy through certain additions."[42]

In the early modern era, there were several Catholic thinkers who defended more thoroughgoing theories of revision of church teaching over time. Cardinal Denis Pétau (Dionysius Petavius), a Jesuit from France who enjoyed a quiet legacy of Ignatian-Thomistic reflection on development, wrote a massive, unfinished *Dogmata Theologica* (1644–50), laying out the most extensive treatment to date of pedagogical refinements to the faith once delivered and showing along the way that much patristic instruction proved deficient by the standards of more recent church history.[43] Johann Sebastian von Drey, a German Catholic and founder of the Catholic theological school in Tübingen, adopted a historicist approach to dogmatics and changes in the Catholic Church's teachings through history, exemplified in Drey's early, unpublished lectures, "Ideen zur Geschichte des Katholischen Dogmensystems" (1812–13).[44] Johann Adam Möhler, a German Catholic priest, Drey's colleague in Tübingen, and an ardent ecumenist, published what became a standard history of doctrine, *Symbolik: Oder Darstellung der dogmatischen Gegensätze der Katholiken und Protestanten nach ihren öffentlichen Bekenntnisschriften* (1832).[45] It represented a trend gaining ground in the West to cultivate biological conceptions of church history, organic understandings of

42. Aquinas, *Summa Theologiae* I, q. 36, a. 2; trans. at New Advent, https://www.newadvent.org/summa/1036.htm.

43. Dionysius Petavius, *Dogmata Theologica*, 5 vols. (Paris: Sebastianus Cramoisy, 1644–50), an unfinished work that went through numerous editions with several volume totals.

44. Johann Sebastian von Drey, "Ideen zur Geschichte des Katholischen Dogmensystems" (1812–13), in *Nachgelassene Schriften*, ed. Max Seckler, 4 vols. (Tübingen: Francke Verlag, 1997–2015), vol. 4.

45. Johann Adam Möhler, *Symbolik: Oder Darstellung der dogmatischen Gegensätze der Katholiken und Protestanten nach ihren öffentlichen Bekenntnisschriften* (Mainz: F. Kupferberg, 1832), trans. James Burton Robertson as *Symbolism, or Exposition of the Doctrinal Differences between Catholics and Protestants and Evidenced by Their Symbolical Writings* (London: Charles Dolman, 1843).

change through time, and it demonstrated clearly that the study of development could aid Catholic thinkers in their conversation with Protestants. This scholarship would not make a difference in parish life for many years to come. It did prepare a way, though, for better-known theories of doctrinal development that captured the attention of the bishops at Vatican II.

Newman was familiar with all of this history. He recognized the power of the *semper eadem* notion and knew that it prevailed among Catholics in his day, most of whom thought that doctrinal variation meant weakness and confusion, not strength and specificity. The sturdiness and stabilizing force of Catholic teaching, indeed, played a role in Newman's own move to Rome. He was no modern liberal. Still, he came of age in a time and place enthralled with evolution, progress, and change, at least along the corridors of academic power. Bishop Bossuet had proved to be the last great apologist to champion *semper eadem*. Even England's Bishop Butler, whose *Analogy of Religion* (1736)—an Anglican defense of revelation and providence admired by Newman—came before the rise of historicism, commended Christianity in progressive doctrinal terms.[46] Newman breathed such thinking in the very air around him. Yet he also valorized the catholic faith once delivered, both in theory and in practice, with great sophistication. This helps us to see why his *Essay* (1845) on development has proven so important to so many faithful Christians, especially in the wake of its adoption by leaders of the Roman magisterium. It offers believers a way of owning up to catechetical change over time without losing faith in special revelation or the churches' teaching ministries.

Newman's *Essay* emerged from deep psychological turmoil. As an adolescent he was converted to a Calvinistic, low-church, evangelical Anglicanism, but his study of church history and friendships in Oxford later drew him to the benefits of ancient church tradition—for

---

46. Joseph Butler, *The Analogy of Religion, Natural and Revealed, to the Constitution and Course of Nature* (Dublin: J. Jones for George Ewing, 1736), a work appreciated by Newman despite its author's latitudinarianism.

doctrinal assurance, liturgical direction, practical instruction, and devotional support. He spent the 1830s and early 1840s nurturing a high-church, catholic sensibility. But even on the eve of his reception into the Catholic Church (1845), he struggled with objections to Roman faith and practice. Most importantly, he wrestled with the question whether the most recent Catholic accessions—with respect to the papacy and Blessed Virgin Mary—were warranted in Scripture and ancient Christian practice. And his work in the *Essay* on what he labeled seven "notes," or "tests," of continuity through doctrinal expansion convinced him that those accessions were warranted—and that *all* the noblest truths of the faith had been refined through the history of the church's teaching ministry. "Time is necessary for the full comprehension and perfection of great ideas," he concluded. "The highest and most wonderful truths, though communicated to the world once for all by inspired teachers, could not be comprehended all at once by the recipients, but, as being received and transmitted by minds not inspired and through media which were human, have required only the longer time and deeper thought for their full elucidation. This may be called the *Theory of Development of Doctrine*."[47] This theory carried Newman all the way across the Tiber. "The Christianity of history is not Protestantism," he argued after decades of distress. "This is shown in the determination" of all too many Protestants to "[dispense] with historical Christianity altogether" and to "[form] a Christianity from the Bible alone." The turmoil of his early years was settled by an oft-quoted statement in the *Essay*: "To be deep in history is to cease to be a Protestant."[48]

Newman's challenge in the *Essay* was to formulate criteria by which we might distinguish good from bad catechetical adjustments over time. Or to put this in his own words, "I venture to set down seven Notes of varying cogency, independence and applicability, to

47. John Henry Newman, *An Essay on the Development of Christian Doctrine*, 6th ed., Notre Dame Series in the Great Books (Notre Dame, IN: University of Notre Dame Press, 1989), 29–30.
48. Newman, *Essay on the Development of Christian Doctrine*, 7–8.

discriminate healthy developments of an idea from its state of corruption and decay." Newman's notes were as follows: (1) a doctrine should be the same sort of teaching in maturity as it was in its infancy (Newman labeled this principle "preservation of type"); (2) "a development, to be faithful, must retain both the doctrine and the principle with which it started" ("continuity of principles"); (3) the most recent iteration of a doctrine should be able to unite the various elements within its evolution ("power of assimilation"); (4) a doctrine "is likely to be a true development, not a corruption, in proportion as it seems to be the *logical* issue of its original teaching" ("logical sequence"); (5) a modern doctrine is salutary insofar as its ancient versions adumbrated its meaning ("anticipation of its future"); (6) developments "which do but contradict and reverse the course of doctrine which has been developed before them . . . are certainly corrupt; for a corruption is a development in that very state in which it ceases to illustrate, and begins to disturb, the acquisitions gained in its previous history" ("conservative action upon its past"); and (7) corruptions usually sprout up quickly and wither, while faithful developments emerge more slowly and stand the test of time ("chronic vigour"). Taken together, these tests ensured essential continuity amid alterations in the churches' teaching ministries and gave modern scholars tools to map continuity throughout the morphologies they studied in the history of Christian doctrine. If not for its forthright admission of adjustments in Catholic catechesis, the *Essay* would have won the day within the magisterium more easily.[49]

As it happened, though, Newman's theory of development would garner more attention on the eve of Vatican II than it did in the century after he published the *Essay*. Not until the rise of the *nouvelle théologie* did leading Catholic thinkers begin to echo its sentiments. (Most of them at first worked within religious orders like the Society of Jesus. Only later did their views gain sanction from bishops.)

---

49. Newman, *Essay on the Development of Christian Doctrine*, 169–206.

In the meantime, moreover, a controversy erupted over what the magisterium condemned as "modernism," a heresy whose principles stemmed from progressive understandings of world history and led to departures from Catholic orthodoxy. As we saw in chapter 1, there were some Catholic thinkers in the late nineteenth and early twentieth centuries for whom "the Tradition" took on a life of its own, exerting preternatural pressure on the history of the church, and was used to establish more radical revisions to Catholic faith and practice than the bishops allowed. Maurice Blondel spoke for many of these more progressive thinkers in his *History and Dogma* (1904), defining the Tradition in a nontraditional way. "Contrary to the vulgar notion," Blondel contended, "we must say that Tradition is not a simple substitute for a written teaching."

> It has a different purpose; it does not proceed solely from it and it does not end by becoming identified with it. . . . Even where we have the Scriptures, it always has something to add, and what passes little by little into writing and definitions is derived from it. It relies, no doubt, on texts, but at the same time it relies primarily on something else, on an experience always in act which enables it to remain in some respects master of the texts instead of being strictly subservient to them.[50]

Blondel's agential Tradition was greater than the aggregate of texts and ancient practices preserved by the Church. It had a proactive spirit that continued to animate Christian faith and practice and explained—and suffused—an open-ended development of doctrine. "A truly supernatural teaching," Blondel reasoned, "is only viable and conceivable if the initial gift is a seed capable of progressive and continual growth. The divine and human Word of Christ did not fix itself in immobility. Jesus wrote only in the sand and impressed his words

---

50. Maurice Blondel, *"The Letter on Apologetics" and "History and Dogma,"* trans. Alexander Dru and Illtyd Trethowan (New York: Holt, Rinehart and Winston, 1964), 267.

only on the air." What conservatives called the deposit of the faith "can only be understood and assimilated, little by little, if nourished by the sources of the moral life and by the suggestions of the invisible Spirit present in every age and in every civilization." The implication was clear for those with ears to hear: "So far is 'development' from being heterodox, as so many believers fear, that it is the static idea of tradition, *fixism*, which is the virtual heresy—whether the static conception is that of the historian who claims to seize the truth of Revelation in its earliest version, or that of the speculative theologian, ready to confine infinite reality in a completed synthesis, as though at some given moment in history the spirit of man had exhausted God's spirit."[51] As readers should expect by this point in our story, such writing raised hackles in Rome.

For years, popes and bishops had resisted progressive understandings of church teaching. Their two most recent church councils, in fact, had featured such resistance. At Trent, the purported improvements of the Protestants had met condemnation. More recently, at Vatican I, so-called advances made by Catholic intellectuals had also been quashed. "That meaning of the sacred dogmas is ever to be maintained," the council fathers warned, "which has once been declared by holy mother church," and "if anyone says that it is possible that at some time, given the advancement of knowledge, a sense may be assigned to the dogmas propounded by the church which is different from that which the church has understood and understands: let him be anathema."[52] In the early twentieth century, despite clear canons and decrees from these councils, Pope Pius X still worried that developmental views were breeding error. In pronouncements like *Lamentabili Sane* (1907) and the more comprehensive *Pascendi Dominici Gregis* (1907), he excoriated scholars who promoted evolutionary views of Christian doctrine and called on the bishops to

---

51. Blondel, *"Letter on Apologetics" and "History and Dogma,"* 275.
52. First Vatican Council, session 3, April 24, 1870, in Tanner, *Decrees of the Ecumenical Councils,* 2:809, 811.

suppress them. "It is not enough to hinder the reading and the sale of bad books," he declared;

> it is also necessary to prevent them from being printed. Hence let the Bishops use the utmost severity in granting permission to print. . . . In all episcopal Curias, . . . let censors be appointed for the revision of works intended for publication, and let the censors be chosen from both ranks of the clergy—secular and regular—men of age, knowledge and prudence who will know how to follow the golden mean in their judgments.[53]

The future looked bleak for developmentalists.

By the 1940s, though, a cadre of churchmen, most of whom were born near the dawn of the century and went on to play important roles at Vatican II, sought to spark a renewal in the Church's teaching ministry with help from the history of doctrine. They called their revitalization effort *ressourcement* (a "return to the sources" for help moving forward). Appealing to the Scriptures and early church fathers, they called Catholic teachers to less scholastic and defensive, more spiritual, biblical, historical instruction. They taught that Christian doctrine had developed over time under the guidance of the Spirit and the Church's teaching office and hoped that such faithful refinement would continue. Like Blondel before them, these Catholic intellectuals—Henri de Lubac, Yves Congar, Karl Rahner, Jean Daniélou, Hans Urs von Balthasar, and others—made use of the concept of capital-*T* Tradition, but not in support of reforms the Church opposed (at least not in the main—they proved more careful when advocating controversial matters). They majored on historical-theological accounts of the Church's faith and practice, nourishing the faithful in the ancient and ever-living witness of God's people. They were blamed by some for modernism in disguise (most famously by Reginald Garrigou-Lagrange,

---

53. Pius X, *Pascendi Dominici Gregis: Encyclical of Pope Pius X on the Doctrines of the Modernists*, ¶52, available at the Vatican website, https://www.vatican.va/content/pius-x/en/encyclicals /documents/hf_p-x_enc_19070908_pascendi-dominici-gregis.html.

a conservative Dominican).[54] But they paved a way for widespread acceptance of the notion that doctrines develop in orthodox fashion.

This notion was embraced by the bishops at Vatican II. In *Dei Verbum* they declared quite clearly, "This tradition which comes from the apostles progresses in the church under the assistance of the holy Spirit. There is a growth in the understanding of what is handed on, both the words and the realities they signify."

This comes about through contemplation and study by believers . . . and through the preaching of those who, on succeeding to the office of bishop, receive the sure charism of truth. Thus, as the centuries advance, the church constantly holds its course towards the fullness of God's truth, until the day when the words of God reach their fulfilment in the church.

The fathers of the church bear witness to the enlivening presence of this tradition, and show how its riches flow into the practice and life of the believing and praying church. By this tradition comes the church's knowledge of the full canon of biblical books; by this too, the scripture itself comes to be more profoundly understood and to realise its power in the church. In this way the God who spoke of old still maintains an uninterrupted conversation with the bride of his beloved Son. The holy Spirit, too, is active, making the living voice of the gospel ring out in the church, and through it in the world, leading those who believe into the whole truth, and making the message of Christ dwell in them in all its richness (see Col. 3:16).[55]

54. Start with Reginald Garrigou-Lagrange, "La Nouvelle Théologie Où Va-t-Elle?," *Angelicum* 23, no. 3/4 (1946): 126–45, which criticized proponents of *ressourcement* only insofar as they advocated developmental views; trans. available as "Where Is the New Theology Leading Us?," Internet Archive, https://web.archive.org/web/20131004223423/http://www.cfnews.org/gg-newtheo .htm. Bear in mind that this champion of "strict observance Thomism" produced many catechetical works of his own, making pedagogical use of the history of doctrine. See, for example, Reginald Garrigou-Lagrange, *Predestination*, trans. Dom Bede Rose (St. Louis: B. Herder, 1939; orig. *La prédestination des saints et la grâce: Doctrine de Saint Thomas comparée aux autres systèmes théologiques* [1936]), available at Internet Archive, https://archive.org/stream/Garrigou-LagrangeEnglish/Pre destination%20-%20Garrigou-Lagrange%2C%20Reginald%2C%20O.P__djvu.txt.

55. Second Vatican Council, session 8, November 18, 1965, in Tanner, *Decrees of the Ecumenical Councils*, 2:974.

As confirmed in the *Catechism of the Catholic Church* (1992), "No new public revelation is to be expected before the glorious manifestation of our Lord Jesus Christ. Yet even if Revelation is already complete, it has not been made completely explicit; it remains for Christian faith gradually to grasp its full significance over the course of the centuries. . . . Thanks to the assistance of the Holy Spirit, the understanding of both the realities and the words of the heritage of faith is able to grow in the life of the Church."[56]

From the time of Newman's *Essay* to the end of Vatican II (120 years), the Catholic magisterium moved from denying the existence and utility of doctrinal revision to taking it for granted and leading it themselves. Not only did the bishops develop Catholic teaching in a transparent fashion at the Second Vatican Council. They proceeded to sanction further work on development, much of it informed by non-Catholic realities, and changed the Church's posture toward the world. Popes like Benedict XVI taught that God continues to speak to his people in and through the Tradition, interpreted authoritatively by the bishops.[57] The Congregation for the Doctrine of the Faith specified, "It sometimes happens that some dogmatic truth is first expressed incompletely (but not falsely), and at a later date, when considered in a broader context of faith or human knowledge, it receives a fuller and more perfect expression."

> Ancient dogmatic formulas and others closely connected with them remain living and fruitful in the habitual usage of the Church, but with suitable expository and explanatory additions that maintain and clarify their original meaning. In addition, it has sometimes happened that in this habitual usage of the Church certain of these formulas gave way to

56. *Catechismus Catholicae Ecclesiae*, part 1, section 1, article 2; trans., *Catechism of the Catholic Church*, 29–35, available at the Vatican website, http://www.vatican.va/archive/ENG0015/_INDEX.HTM.

57. This doctrine is taught in Joseph Ratzinger [Pope Benedict XVI], *Wort Gottes: Schrift-Tradition-Amt* (Freiburg im Breisgau: Herder, 2005); trans., *God's Word: Scripture-Tradition-Office*, ed. Peter Hünermann and Thomas Söding (San Francisco: Ignatius, 2008).

new expressions which, proposed and approved by the Sacred Magisterium, presented more clearly or more completely the same meaning.[58]

Theologians like the Belgian priest Jan Hendrik Walgrave, a noted Newman scholar, wrote standard scholarly treatments of doctrinal development employed by Catholics and non-Catholics alike. "Although nothing new is added to the deposit of faith since the closing of apostolic times," he affirmed, "it may be said that the living process of revelation goes on till the end of time. God has completed His self-communication in Christ. But revelation is not only something that proceeds from God. It has to be received in the human mind. The process through which the mind of the Church is penetrated by the Word of God, leading to a progressive understanding of all its implications, can go on as long as history lasts."[59] Cardinals would be made of the likes of Avery Dulles, who produced a taxonomy of developmental views in Catholic Church history—"logical," "organic," and "situationist," he termed them—and registered a preference for approaches to development marked by responsiveness to changes in the world outside the Catholic Church (i.e., situationist).[60] Catholic organizations that serve the Holy See would even use Newman's notes to shine a light upon the ways in which "Christianity's taking root" in new cultural contexts expands the tradition and contributes to its teaching.[61] Almost no one saw this coming in 1900.

58. Congregation for the Doctrine of the Faith, *Mysterium Ecclesiae: Declaration in Defense of the Catholic Doctrine on the Church against Certain Errors of the Present Day* (1973), 5, available at the Vatican website, https://www.vatican.va/roman_curia/congregations/cfaith/documents/rc_con_cfaith_doc_19730705_mysterium-ecclesiae_en.html.

59. Jan Hendrik Walgrave, *Unfolding Revelation: The Nature of Doctrinal Development*, Theological Resources (Philadelphia: Westminster, 1972), 46.

60. Avery Dulles, *The Resilient Church: The Necessity and Limits of Adaptation* (Garden City, NY: Doubleday, 1977), 48–52.

61. International Theological Commission, "On the Interpretation of Dogmas," trans. Carl Peter [from German], *Origins: CNS Documentary Service* 20 (May 17, 1990): 1–15. The International Theological Commission is an institution of the Roman Catholic Church whose task is to help the Holy See and primarily the Congregation for the Doctrine of the Faith in examining doctrinal questions of major importance.

Protestant Communions

In the Protestant communions, the question whether doctrine should ever be revised is an easy one to answer: yes, all agree, on the basis of the Word as interpretations of Scripture continue to improve and new questions arise amid the contexts in which Christianity is practiced. But agreement stops there. The frequency with which church teaching should develop, the burden of proof on those who contend for doctrinal change, the ongoing force of ancient creeds and confessions, and the leaders responsible for doctrinal development have long been debated by the heirs of Luther.

During the Reformation itself, many doctrines were revised—in many different ways—by the Protestant divines. Most important were the well-known Reformation *solas*, especially justification by grace through faith alone (without regard to merit) and the doctrine that the Bible is the only norm that norms the rest, the ultimate authority on matters of faith and practice (over popes, other bishops, and ecclesiastical councils). There were several other doctrines, though, that came in for revision, most of which pertained to the church and its sacraments. The Lutherans hewed closest to inherited formulations. The Reformed engaged in rather more extensive reconstruction. The Anabaptists proved most revisionist of all. But all of them promoted what they called the Scripture principle, the notion that ideas not spelled out in the Bible should not be inculcated as matters of faith and practice. And most of them developed new confessional materials that codified their churches' central teachings. Indeed, even radical reformers who favored new slogans like "no creed but the Bible" wound up publishing synopses of their doctrine.[62]

In the age of the Enlightenment, some Protestant intellectuals became freethinkers with little or no love for official church teaching.

---

62. See Karl Koop, *Anabaptist-Mennonite Confessions of Faith: The Development of a Tradition*, Anabaptist and Mennonite Studies (Kitchener, ON: Pandora Press, 2004), who notes, paradoxically, that Anabaptists "may have actually produced more confessions than any other Reformation tradition" (11).

They encouraged Western Christians to think for themselves. They opposed the authority of ecclesiastical leaders. They advocated criticism of most church traditions. And thus they made a bigger difference outside of the churches—in the modern universities and "republic of letters"—than they did within the churches and their pedagogical ministries. Thomas Hobbes, John Locke, Jean LeClerc, David Hume, Immanuel Kant, and their ilk would eventually shape the pedagogy of many liberal Protestants. They have had less influence, at least so far, on the use of creeds, confessions, and other catechetical tools to shape the faith of more traditional believers.

The eagerness of Protestants to "get back to the Bible" and encourage lay Christians to read it for themselves, though, has generated tensions in the churches through the centuries—tensions raised further by the rise of freethinking—over just what kinds of authority creeds and confessions ought to have. Such tensions have arisen all over the Protestant world. They have caused the most concern in North America, however, where many church leaders have worried about handing on confessional identities, forged in the fires of "old-world" ethnic histories, in "new-world" contexts with much different histories and demographics. The most stringent authorities have sought strict subscription to confessions by their clergy and detailed adherence to the language of these teaching tools "because" (*quia*) they epitomize the contents of the Bible. Pietistic Protestants have proven more flexible. Opposed to "dead orthodoxy" and anxious to avoid a reputation for hypocrisy, they have held confessions lightly, adhering to them only "for the substance of their doctrine" and only "insofar as" (*quatenus*) they accurately synopsize the main themes of Scripture. Nearly every Protestant group has had its own confessional row over just how strictly the clergy should adhere to their statements of faith. The subscription debates among the early Presbyterians and later German Lutherans who settled in America are but the best known. These were usually family feuds among fellow believers intent on nurturing the faith once delivered. Before the nineteenth century, they rarely had to do with alterations to the teaching tools themselves.

As noted already, though, the nineteenth century brought with it winds of change. The rise of historicism, evolutionary understandings of world history, and romantic conceptions of the immanence of God in the patterns of history and organic maturation of the body of Christ on earth led to new ways of thinking about the nature and history of doctrine, even among traditionalists. Some Protestant leaders made changes to their teaching tools, updating them to meet the needs of the day. Others now relativized their creeds and confessions, approaching all summaries of Christian faith and practice as "symbols" of the faith of those who first wrote and taught them and studying the history of these symbols in view of a desire to resymbolize the faith in every age, continuing the work of reforming God's people on the basis of the Word. This opened the door to a host of new confessions, some of which featured more liberal construals of age-old doctrines and most of which emphasized ethical entailments of the faith for modern Christians. (The ecumenical movement and decolonization of the Christian global south, both of which would flourish in the century to come, yielded even more statements, giving voice simultaneously to those who sought unity across denominations and those who sought to speak the faith in their own terms.) Some conservatives opposed this, concerned that the *semper reformanda* idea would engender infidelity dressed up as relevance. But most heirs of Luther came to feel that their leaders should communicate the Word of God afresh in every age, not parroting the talking points of bygone ages, but paraphrasing the faith once delivered to the saints in terminology compelling to contemporaries.

The best-known Protestant traditionalists to navigate these winds were the Mercersburg men John Nevin and Philip Schaff. Though they lived in a tiny town in central Pennsylvania and served a small assortment of German Reformed churches, they straddled the tensions of their age with erudition, honesty, and courage, repackaging their faith in a controversial manner but representing famously the challenges engaged by those who sought to convey ancient knowledge codified in statements made (for Protestants) in early modern Europe in a brave, new, globalizing world. Nevin came of age before the rise of historicism and underwent a spiritual awakening of sorts to developmental views of the church's formation.[63] Schaff came of age under the influence of much more historically minded teachers in German-speaking Europe. But both men championed the development of doctrine. In *What Is Church History? A Vindication of the Idea of Historical Development* (1846), Schaff made claims that sound a lot like Newman, right after Newman published his *Essay* on development (1845). "So precisely as the single Christian does not become complete at a stroke," Schaff contended, "but only by degrees, the Church, as the complex of all Christians, must admit and require too a gradual development." Such incremental growth "is *organic*," moreover.

> It is no mechanical accumulation of events, and no result simply of foreign influences. Certain outward conditions are indeed required for it, as the plant needs air, moisture, and light, in order to grow. But still the impelling force in the process, is the inmost life of the church herself. Christianity is a new creation, that unfolds itself continually more and more from within, and extends itself by the necessity of its own nature. It takes up, it is true, foreign material also, in the process; but changes it at once into its own spirit, and assimilates it to its own nature, as the body converts the food, required for its growth, into flesh and blood, marrow and bone.[64]

For Nevin and Schaff, Christian growth ends only at the eschaton. Until that time, the church's teachers would struggle in the providence

---

63. John W. Nevin, *My Own Life: The Earlier Years*, Papers of the Eastern Chapter, Historical Society of the Evangelical and Reformed Church (Lancaster, PA: Historical Society of the Evangelical and Reformed Church, 1964; published orig. in 17 installments of the *Reformed Church Messenger*, March 2 to June 22, 1870), 40.

64. Philip Schaff, *What Is Church History? A Vindication of the Idea of Historical Development*, trans. John W. Nevin (Philadelphia: J. B. Lippincott and Co., 1846), 87, 91.

of God to improve their catechesis in light of new knowledge and cultural experience. Or as Schaff said in *History of the Apostolic Church* (1853), their teaching would "change with the spirit and culture of the age; whereas the Biblical truth in itself continues always the same, though ever fresh and ever new. Each period of church history is called to unfold and place in clear light a particular aspect of the doctrine, to counteract a corresponding error; till the whole circle of Christian truth shall have been traversed in its natural order."[65] A more forceful endorsement of doctrinal revision for nineteenth-century Christians is hard to conceive.

Most conventional Protestant pedagogues since that time have embraced the Scripture principle and disagreed with those who treat capital-*T* Tradition as a force of its own in the development of doctrine. They have differed among themselves about the role of church history in Christian catechesis. Some have granted creeds, confessions, and traditions a presumptive authority in guiding exegesis and, thus, doctrinal instruction. Others have assumed that such man-made constructions are by definition faulty, unstable, and in need of either regular revision or, sometimes, replacement. But everyone has taught that all pedagogical change should be based upon the Word. And especially in the twentieth and twenty-first centuries, many have stressed the role that new Bible translations and cross-cultural missions can play in improving our instruction in the churches.

Vanhoozer's work has brought together many faithful Protestants, articulating a broad evangelical consensus on the nature, history, and development of doctrine. In *Theology and the Mirror of Scripture* (2015), written with Daniel Treier, he has represented the thought of the bulk of his community about the issues at hand in an ecumenical spirit. "All the treasures of wisdom are in Jesus Christ," the authors note, reproducing Saint Paul (Col. 2:3). "However, just as it took four Gospels to set forth his narrative identity in speech, so it may take

---

65. Philip Schaff, *History of the Apostolic Church, with a General Introduction to Church History*, trans. Edward D. Yeomans, rev. ed. (New York: Scribner, Armstrong, 1874; orig. 1853), 22.

many interpretations—communicated and lived—to embody the wisdom potential that is in Christ. . . . Scripture is sufficient, yet it takes four Evangelists to tell the story of Jesus Christ. In similar fashion, could it not take a number of different voices (denominations, cultures, even eras) to articulate all the wisdom and blessings that are in Christ?"[66] With most serious Protestants since the sixteenth century, Vanhoozer and Treier hold firmly to the Bible as the final authority for Christian faith and practice while stressing that it takes a whole village or, better, the entire body of Christ to interpret and perform it convincingly. And like most serious Protestants since the nineteenth century, they also underscore the global nature of the church and the benefits of intercultural work on Christian doctrine: "Crosscultural mission is itself an exercise in doctrinal development. . . . Mission—setting forth in word, deed and presence what is in Christ—becomes an exercise in doctrinal development whenever a different language, whether of a different culture, social class or even ecclesial tradition, is involved. Every attempt to cross cultural borders requires theological wisdom: the ability to go on in the same Way of Jesus Christ in new situations."[67] As these comments make clear, missiologists like those we discussed in chapter 2 have now moved to the mainstream. Today, most Christians—Orthodox, Catholic, and Protestant—celebrate the blessings of identifying and handing on the faith once delivered with the whole body of Christ, past and present, near and far.

Why Does Any of This Matter?

Why does any of this matter? many laypeople ask. What does it have to do with my everyday life in the home, workplace, or local church? It has *everything* to do with the love of God and neighbor—good

66. Kevin J. Vanhoozer and Daniel J. Treier, *Theology and the Mirror of Scripture: A Mere Evangelical Account*, Studies in Christian Doctrine and Scripture (Downers Grove, IL: IVP Academic, 2015), 121–22.

67. Vanhoozer and Treier, *Theology and the Mirror of Scripture*, 120–21.

teachers should reply—everything to do with the tenor and trajectory of daily discipleship. When we view Christian doctrine as what is taught in our churches to shape faith and practice, and we recognize that getting doctrine right will require us to move with godly wisdom from ancient revelation (the deposit of the faith) to Christian catechesis (received from our elders and handed on to others) to everyday behavior—when we care about the way in which we live day by day in response to God's will as discerned by his people—we appreciate efforts to learn and make good use of the history of our teaching. We see that this history affects Christian living (for better or for worse) by the worldwide people of God (whether they know it or not).

This pastoral, practical, prudential understanding of the functions of doctrine and doctrinal history has been underscored in recent years by many different writers, several of them women. In *By the Renewing of Your Minds: The Pastoral Function of Christian Doctrine* (1997), Ellen Charry of the Perkins School of Divinity reminds us that "Christian doctrines aim to be good for us by forming or reforming our character. . . . When Christian doctrines assert the truth about God, the world, and ourselves," she continued, "it is a truth that seeks to influence us."[68] Beth Felker Jones of Wheaton College has phrased this matter more simply. In *Practicing Christian Doctrine: An Introduction to Thinking and Living Theologically* (2014), she contends that "beliefs must be put into practice, and faithful practice matters for what we believe." As if incentivizing this, she assures faithful readers, "When we connect truth with action and doctrine with discipleship, God does marvelous things." In fact, "the study of doctrine is an act of love for God: in studying the things of God, we are formed as worshipers and as God's servants in the world."[69] What could possibly be more important than that?

68. Ellen T. Charry, *By the Renewing of Your Minds: The Pastoral Function of Christian Doctrine* (New York: Oxford University Press, 1997), vii–viii.
69. Beth Felker Jones, *Practicing Christian Doctrine: An Introduction to Thinking and Living Theologically* (Grand Rapids: Baker Academic, 2014), 2–3.

Earnest disciples, moreover, have always sought instruction delivered by people who are loyal to the best of the church's own history.
Long before the Bible was a gleam in the eyes of the early church
fathers, believers "devoted themselves to the apostles' teaching and
fellowship, to the breaking of bread and the prayers" (Acts 2:42).
And as time wore on, they were cautioned to "guard" the instruction
they received (1 Tim. 6:20) and build upon that teaching—and only
that teaching—as they lived out their faith (1 Cor. 3:10–15). As Paul
exhorted Timothy, "Hold to the standard of sound teaching that you
have heard from me. . . . Guard the good treasure entrusted to you"
(2 Tim. 1:13–14); and, "What you have heard from me through many
witnesses entrust to faithful people who will be able to teach others" (2:2). Ancient Christians understood this as a matter of life and
death. For as Peter warned readers about the peril of false teachers,
"It would have been better for them never to have known the way
of righteousness than, after knowing it, to turn back from the holy
commandment that was passed on to them" (2 Pet. 2:21).

From the Lord's Great Commission to go and make disciples,
"teaching them to obey everything that I have commanded you" (Matt.
28:20), to the preaching and writing of the New Testament authors,
to the work of the early church fathers and apologists, Jesus' first followers prioritized instruction steeped in the faith once delivered to
the saints. We should do no less. For as Paul put the matter in a letter
to the Corinthians, "I should remind you, brothers and sisters, of the
good news that I proclaimed to you, which you in turn received, in
which also you stand, through which also you are being saved, if you
hold firmly to the message that I proclaimed to you" (1 Cor. 15:1–2).
Holding firmly to the message has always been important. Conveying it to others has been more important. "Stand firm and hold fast
to the traditions that you were taught by us," Paul advised frequently
(2 Thess. 2:15), commending his students for "maintain[ing] the traditions just as I handed them on to you" (1 Cor. 11:2). Thoroughgoing efforts to inculcate the Christian faith across time and space,

inspiring devotion to its foremost traditions, are rooted in the soil of the Scriptures.

In my fourth and final chapter, I will bring this story all the way to the present, showing what is at stake in the ways in which we understand and teach Christian doctrine to the faithful today. I will scan the leading ways in which contemporary teachers make use of the history of our faith in their work, and I will conclude with suggestions for those who want to serve as better teachers in the future.

4

Teaching in, with, and under
the Christian Church

Thus says the Lord: Stand at the crossroads, and look, and ask for the ancient paths, where the good way lies; and walk in it, and find rest for your souls.

—Jeremiah 6:16

But we must always give thanks to God for you, brothers and sisters beloved by the Lord, because God chose you as the first fruits for salvation through sanctification by the Spirit and through belief in the truth. For this purpose he called you through our proclamation of the good news, so that you may obtain the glory of our Lord Jesus Christ. So then, brothers and sisters, stand firm and hold fast to the traditions that you were taught by us, either by word of mouth or by our letter.

—2 Thessalonians 2:13–15

You then, my child, be strong in the grace that is in Christ Jesus; and what you have heard from me through many witnesses entrust to faithful people who will be able to teach others as well.

—2 Timothy 2:1–2

Let us hold fast to the confession of our hope without wavering, for he who has promised is faithful. And let us consider how to provoke one another to love and good deeds, not neglecting to meet together, as is the habit of some, but encouraging one another, and all the more as you see the Day approaching.

—Hebrews 10:23–25

There are many different ways in which serious disciples make use of the history of Christian doctrine today. Some are better organized and thematized than others. A few are quite famous. And most have been informed by late-modern scholarship on the notion of tradition and its role in shaping everyday belief and behavior. Of course, many church leaders do their work independently, largely unaware of both the history and present-day practice of the worldwide church's teaching ministries. And some who pay attention to the issues handled here have their own ways of inculcating Christian faith and practice, ways that fit poorly in the usual taxonomies. In what follows we will look at but the best-known ways, reviewing them in light of recent work on tradition. My aim is not to be exhaustive but to spark better thinking on the task of Christian pedagogy across time and space. I will end with suggestions for handing on the faith in, with, and under the church—with the entire body of Christ, past and present, at home and abroad—in the decades to come.

Another word about our remit before we begin: Many now assume that promoting the use of history in Christian catechesis is tantamount to advocating Eurocentric teaching, especially when the history at issue is doctrinal. But most of the teachers we will survey in this chapter are alert to the global nature of the Christian church. Many of them are keen to include non-Western Christian voices in their teaching. In fact, some have concluded that to do so well requires a major deconstruction of the canons of Scripture and the doctors of the church used to teach Christian faith to the next generation. Nearly all know the challenges of handing on the faith in a multicultural way without undermining trust in ecclesiastical unity. The present author wrestles with such challenges profoundly. If the church is really one, holy, catholic, and apostolic, as most of us confess, then there must be a way to advance both oneness and diversity together—to be traditional *and* global. May God help us as we find that way together.

"Constructive Theology" and Its Liberating Pedagogy

Our first approach to making use of doctrinal history in contemporary teaching usually goes by the name of "constructive theology." Most who take this approach are progressive Protestants or morally driven former Christians who now express their faith in largely secular academic and other social contexts. But some are Roman Catholic. And many of the emphases and methods pioneered by its best-known practitioners are shared by a wide range of other theologians who work primarily in higher education.

Its emphases and methods emerged long ago, in the age of the Enlightenment. Antiauthoritarian critics of received views of Scripture and tradition raised questions about the inspiration, authority, coherence, and mores of the Bible and mainstream traditions of Christian faith and practice. They argued that Scripture and tradition were more human, fallible, and sometimes even harmful than assumed. They encouraged all who listened to discard the dead weight of these burdensome authorities, think for themselves, and teach the faith moving forward in a way that was better for themselves and those they served. The Enlightenment, they taught, had revolutionized the teaching of religion in the present. It had freed Christian teachers from the tutelage of those who had not served their interests, enabling them to make new models of God and God's relation to the world that were liberating for those long oppressed by the church. By the nineteenth century, new words were invented to refer to this approach: *Neuprotestantismus*—in English, neo-Protestantism.

These emphases were nurtured in the late twentieth century by leaders of a loose constellation of scholars called "constructive theologians." Working from a wide array of colleges and seminaries, most importantly Vanderbilt and Harvard Divinity School, these liberal theologians contended that the ancient Christian structures of authority had long since collapsed and that their job as Christian teachers was to let people know, to deconstruct the doctrines that were based on old authorities and used to confine and control other people, and to retrieve from the ruins choice fragments of Scripture and tradition they could use to build new models of God, constructing more liberating pedagogical tools for their people in the present.

The best-known thinkers to develop this approach during the past half century have done so in the Workgroup on Constructive Theology, a multiethnic association of academic thinkers who collaborate on many different projects. This Workgroup has published several books on their priorities, which serve as the finest introduction to their movement. The first of these books appeared in 1982 and was edited by Vanderbilt's Peter C. Hodgson and Robert King of Millsaps College in Mississippi. Its contributors, the editors explained in a preface, approached the Enlightenment "as a critical watershed in the history of theology, demanding new paradigms or models of theological reflection in light of the impact on the tradition of critical methods, new scholarly disciplines, the increasing pluralization and secularization of Western culture, and so forth." Hodgson and Vanderbilt colleague Edward Farley wrote the most important chapter in this groundbreaking volume, "Scripture and Tradition," asserting axiomatically that "the house of authority has collapsed, despite the fact that many people still try to live in it." They rejected "the traditional way of understanding the church as primarily a community of *revelation* that endures by means of deposits of revelation in scripture, dogmas, and institutions." They argued instead that what they called "ecclesial existence" is "the redemptive presence of the transcendent" in the world and that "ecclesial process" (an "utterly historical process, subject to the contingencies, failures, and unfinished character of all such processes") is "the salvific work of God in history." Gone was our ability to know about the work of a personal God in history. Gone were traditionary sources of authority meant to shape Christian teaching across time and space. As Vanderbilt colleague Sallie McFague summarized in the book's epilogue, "The relativization of scripture and tradition, as well as the critique of classical Christianity by the liberation theologies, have raised the question of Christianity's orientation to the past in a serious way." The "future is now seen by many theologians to be more viable than the past as a source for transforming the present. The envisioning of an alternative future . . . creates a critical perspective from which the oppressive structures of the present can be changed."[1]

Three more textbooks appeared from this group over the course of the next few decades.[2] Then in 2016, yet another work, called *Awake to the Moment*, appeared in which a younger generation of twenty-eight members engaged in further definition of constructive theology—and did so seamlessly, without attaching authors' names to chapters or sections. Social justice concerns lie "at the root of what we mean by the term *constructive theology*," these colleagues announced. And this passion only intensified their deconstructive labors on the Bible and tradition. "We are theologians who are not afraid to criticize the role our own religious traditions have played in creating the problems in our world today," they said. "Out of our anger and protest at Christian abuses and out of love of our Christian

---

1. Peter C. Hodgson and Robert H. King, eds., *Christian Theology: An Introduction to Its Traditions and Tasks*, 2nd ed. (Philadelphia: Fortress, 1985; orig. ed. 1982), x, 76, 84, 86, 388.

2. Peter C. Hodgson and Robert H. King, eds., *Readings in Christian Theology* (Minneapolis: Fortress, 1985); Rebecca S. Chopp and Mark Lewis Taylor, eds., *Reconstructing Christian Theology* (Minneapolis: Fortress, 1994); Serene Jones and Paul Lakeland, eds., *Constructive Theology: A Contemporary Approach to Classical Themes*, A Project of the Workgroup on Constructive Christian Theology (Minneapolis: Fortress, 2005).

traditions, we are inspired to engage those traditions more energetically and constructively." They saw scattered "seeds of hope" in the history of doctrine for "a world of peace and justice, a world where racism, sexism, poverty, ecological degradation, and oppression are overcome." But those seeds now required a very different kind of tending, the Workgroup averred. "Many of us feel a sense of weight, constraint, binding, and even a sense of guilt about the grave harms the Christian tradition has directly or indirectly inflicted on countless bodies throughout history," they explained. "The crusades, inquisitions, slavery, and pogroms of the past are repeated in today's global religious conflicts, so for many of us in constructive theology, 'tradition' is not a warm and fuzzy word." On "some days," in fact, the Workgroup groaned, "we want nothing to do with tradition." Then they criticized the churches' hegemonic view of tradition, calling for the recovery of voices from the past that had long been marginalized, ignored, and even muffled but that underwrote their platform of justice and inclusion. They called for "deconstructing the myth of a singular, unadulterated, and internally homogeneous Christian Tradition." They confessed that they too viewed some strands of history as more salutary than others (like everybody else), but insisted on maintaining "the diversity of Christian traditions itself as the norm" and declared "most valid those Christian traditions where love, justice, and flourishing abide." They urged mainstream churches to "question tradition and seek to subvert its mistaken convictions." Only if and when this happened, the authors concluded, would their teachers be freed to reconstruct the tradition in more liberating ways from the margins of church history.[3]

Not many of these writers serve as teachers of the faith in traditional congregations. But most teach students and write for clergy who do.

3. Laurel C. Schneider and Stephen G. Ray Jr., eds., *Awake to the Moment: An Introduction to Theology*, The Workgroup on Constructive Theology (Louisville: Westminster John Knox, 2016), 10–11, 71, 87, 90, 92. Contributors include Wendy Farley, Jeannine Hill Fletcher, Mary McClintock Fulkerson, Joerg Rieger, Mayra Rivera, and John Thatamanil.

"Retrieval Theology" and Its Classical Instruction

Our next approach to making use of doctrinal history in contemporary teaching is "retrieval theology," a term coined recently, mainly in the wake of the constructive theologians, for a loose set of attitudes, practices, and methods that predate the term itself. Most retrieval theologians are traditional Protestants, though some within their networks are Catholic and Orthodox. Many appeal to advocates of *ressourcement*, postliberal theology, and neo-patristic thought as antecedents of their efforts to retrieve Christian wisdom from the past for present purposes.

While constructive theologians retrieve useful fragments from the margins of church history, employing them to reconstruct liberating understandings of God in pursuit of social justice for the oppressed, retrieval theologians rehabilitate the classic texts of mainstream churches, using them to substantiate contemporary versions of traditional dogmatics. They do so in the manner of the history of ideas, engaging texts and doctrines as transhistorical units from the Bible and tradition, treating them as if they have a life of their own that continues to inform Christian teaching today (a method now passé in academic history departments, where ideas are interpreted primarily in relation to their own historical contexts).[4] But like their liberal colleagues in constructive theology, retrieval theologians also criticize, update, and revise the texts and doctrines they engage from the past. And this sets them apart from most older theologians, who taught within the boundaries of their churches and confessions and had less freedom to venture forth on their own. Retrieval theologians do their work most often as teachers in the schools. Many of them are active in the churches as well. But their own "constructive moves" in

4. The "history of ideas" was pioneered by Arthur Lovejoy, who taught at Johns Hopkins University and founded the *Journal of the History of Ideas*. He laid the intellectual groundwork for this way of making good use of intellectual history in Arthur O. Lovejoy, *The Great Chain of Being: A Study of the History of an Idea* (Cambridge, MA: Harvard University Press, 1936); Lovejoy, *Essays in the History of Ideas* (Baltimore: Johns Hopkins University Press, 1948).

response to the classics are the best-known features of their teaching ministries.

The most influential spokesman for retrieval theology is the late John Webster, who devoted his mature years to graduate students in Oxford, Aberdeen, and St. Andrews. Webster championed the virtues of retrieval, explaining that for people like him, "immersion in the texts and habits of thought of earlier (especially pre-modern) theology opens up a wide view of the object of Christian theological reflection, setting before its contemporary practitioners descriptions of the faith unharassed by current anxieties, and enabling a certain liberty in relation to the present." He insisted that his allies involved in retrieval were independent, diverse, and not always conservative. Still, they shared what Webster called "a rough set of resemblances," traits that he itemized in rather traditional terms:

> These theologies are "objectivist" or "realist" insofar as they consider Christian faith and theology to be a response to a self-bestowing divine reality which precedes and overcomes the limited reach of rational intention; their material accounts of this divine reality are heavily indebted to the Trinitarian, incarnational, and soteriological teaching of the classical Christianity of the ecumenical councils; they consider that the governing norms of theological inquiry are established by the object by which theology is brought into being (the source of theology is thus its norm); accordingly they do not accord final weight to external criteria or to the methods and procedures which enjoy prestige outside theology; their accounts of the location, audience, and ends of Christian doctrine are generally governed by the relation of theology to the community of faith as its primary sphere; and in their judgements about the historical setting of systematic theology they tend to deploy a theological (rather than socio-cultural) understanding of tradition which outbids the view that modernity has imposed a new and inescapable set of conditions on theological work.[5]

5. John Webster, "Theologies of Retrieval," in *The Oxford Handbook of Systematic Theology*, ed. John Webster, Kathryn Tanner, and Iain Torrance (New York: Oxford University Press, 2007), 584–85.

In sum, he concluded, "though theologies of retrieval are widely divergent, they entertain a common attitude to the biblical and theological traditions which preceded and enclose contemporary theology: more trustful, more confident in their contemporary serviceability, unpersuaded of the superiority of the present age." They "eschew saying anything new," Webster prodded, "not in the sense that they content themselves with formulaic repetition, still less in endorsing everything the tradition has ever said—but in the sense that they operate on the presupposition that resolutions to the questions which they address may well be found already somewhere in the inheritance of the Christian past."[6]

Shortly after Webster died, his former student Darren Sarisky released a set of essays by a wide array of teachers—Catholic, Orthodox, and Protestant—that featured a comprehensive view of this approach. Emphasizing once again that retrieval theologians were not monolithic, Sarisky allowed that they all mined the past in order to resource creative new work in the present—without apology for majoring in the theological aspects of historic Christian faith. "Theologies of retrieval are less taken up with the conditions of the possibility of Christian theology in the present than they are absorbed by the material content of theology," Sarisky explained. "Theologies of retrieval unsettle present discussions by offering resources from beyond the current horizon with a view toward enriching ongoing debates."[7] After giving voice to many different theological scholars who were willing to be known as retrieval theologians (whether or not they had used this label in the past), he reiterated that all of them explored the great tradition of Christian faith and practice with deep appreciation and did so in the service of their own dogmatic work. "Constructive theological work," Sarisky concluded, "requires adapting what one says to the particular contingent circumstances one is addressing." That "theologians of

6. Webster, "Theologies of Retrieval," 592–93.
7. Darren Sarisky, introduction to *Theologies of Retrieval: An Exploration and Appraisal*, ed. Darren Sarisky (London: T&T Clark, 2017), 2.

retrieval are participants in an ongoing conversation, not outside observers of a discussion being had by others, means that the theologian both listens to the historical sources and articulates her own constructive response to them." Retrieval is not the same, then, as repristination. It is "not about reinstituting large swaths of the past, a whole nexus of interconnected elements of meaning, as much as it is *parts* of it that are considered especially worthy of imitation. In this sense, retrieval involves a selective reading of the past—not in a way that simply confirms what one already thought but that gravitates toward especially promising points that might open up new possibilities for theological reflections." Some retrieval theologians are less interested than this in distinguishing themselves from the elements of catholic tradition they engage. But in the end, most members of this more conventional movement consult the history of doctrine to develop it.[8]

Ressourcement Revisited

It should go without saying at this point in my narrative, but many modern Catholics, especially, plumb the depths of the Christian tradition less in terms of constructive or retrieval theology than of *ressourcement*. And many Orthodox prefer to engage the history of doctrine as neo-Patristic thinkers untethered to the practices of Protestant professors. I assayed these Catholic and Orthodox movements in chapter 3, above. I will not review them here, except to note that their proponents—especially the practitioners of *ressourcement*—have found allies and supporters in the Protestant communions. It can be difficult, indeed, to distinguish the efforts of retrieval theologians from those who identify with *ressourcement*. Both movements mine the past for purchase on the present. Retrieval theologians define their activities most often over against those of modernistic liberals in mainline churches and academic settings. Teachers who identify with

8. Darren Sarisky, "Tradition II: Thinking with Historical Texts—Reflections on Theologies of Retrieval," in Sarisky, *Theologies of Retrieval*, 199, 205–6.

ressourcement define their work most often against old-school, Roman Catholic manual theologians (and major in the writings of the early church fathers more consistently than Protestant retrievalists have done). Catholics and Orthodox are bound more securely than their evangelical colleagues to canons overseen by episcopal authorities. But all of these groups approach the history of doctrine with similar motivations, priorities, and goals.

"Free Church Theologies" in Search of Deeper Roots

Our next constellation of modern-day teachers making use of church history in handing on the faith have fewer creedal and confessional priorities in mind as they probe the history of doctrine. Free-church Protestants oppose impositions of belief from above. They are known for defending congregational autonomy, for emphasizing "the right of private judgment" in the province of Christian faith and practice, and for trademark slogans such as "no creed but the Bible." They appear to most observers to spurn the great tradition when teaching Christian faith, touting Scripture alone as the source of all that matters in the practice of discipleship.

There have long been exceptions to these tendencies, however. And in recent years, especially, a growing number of free-church leaders have been calling for more catholic approaches to handing on the faith. Baptist scholar Daniel Williams of Baylor University catalyzed a free-church return to tradition in landmark writings like *Retrieving the Tradition and Renewing Evangelicalism* (1999), *The Free Church and the Early Church* (2002), and *Evangelicals and Tradition* (2005).[9] He confessed that in the minds of many free-church members, "true believers need only uphold the complete authority of the Bible and

9. D. H. Williams, *Retrieving the Tradition and Renewing Evangelicalism: A Primer for Suspicious Protestants* (Grand Rapids: Eerdmans, 1999); Williams, ed., *The Free Church and the Early Church: Bridging the Historical and Theological Divide* (Grand Rapids: Eerdmans, 2002); Williams, *Evangelicals and Tradition: The Formative Influence of the Early Church*, Evangelical Ressourcement: Ancient Sources for the Church's Future (Grand Rapids: Baker Academic, 2005).

the free working of the Holy Spirit in the life of each individual in order to preserve the 'pattern of sound teaching' (2 Tim. 1:13)." Authentic Christianity, for many such people, "is judged more by one's personal encounter with God, usually the conversion experience, than by conscious participation in an historical and ecclesiological tradition." Unfortunately, moreover, "this individualizing of the faith has often served to disconnect a large number of Christians from the rich and vibrant heritage of the church's common past."[10] Williams urged free-church colleagues to embrace the tradition, deepening their knowledge of the Lord and his Word and strengthening their ties to the rest of the church. An expert in patristics, he argued that "the path of renewal" for his kin "is found through mimicking our earliest Protestant ancestors, namely, by rediscovering the roots in the church's early spirituality and theology."[11]

In the wake of Williams's work, an increasing number of up-and-coming free-church scholars, especially in America,[12] have established a trend toward free-church catholicity. Steven Harmon, for example, a professor at the Baptist Gardner-Webb School of Divinity, has argued that "the reconstruction of the Baptist vision in the wake of modernity's dissolution requires a retrieval of the ancient ecumenical tradition that forms Christian identity through liturgical rehearsal, catechetical instruction, and ecclesial practice. The movement of Baptists towards catholicity," Harmon asserts, "is neither a betrayal of cherished Baptist principles nor the introduction of alien elements into the Baptist tradition." It "is rooted in a recovery of the surprisingly catholic ecclesial outlook of the earliest Baptists, an outlook that has become obscured by more recent modern reinterpretations of the Baptist vision."[13]

10. D. H. Williams, preface to *The Free Church and the Early Church*, viii.

11. D. H. Williams, "Scripture, Tradition, and the Church: Reformation and Post-Reformation," in Williams, *The Free Church and the Early Church*, 126.

12. Of course, other Baptists stump for catholicity as well, most famously the British theologian Stephen Holmes, whose *Listening to the Past: The Place of Tradition in Theology* (Grand Rapids: Baker Academic, 2003), has inspired those mentioned in this paragraph.

13. Steven R. Harmon, *Towards Baptist Catholicity: Essays on Tradition and the Baptist Vision*, Studies in Baptist History and Thought (Milton Keyes, UK: Paternoster, 2006), xix. See

Malcolm Yarnell of Southwestern Baptist Theological Seminary and Gregg Allison of Southern Baptist Theological Seminary have written histories of doctrine and dubbed Christian learning from the past "extremely wise," in the words of Yarnell.[14] "My hope," writes Allison, "is that the church, and evangelicals in particular, will become as familiar with the giants of the past . . . as they are with Billy Graham, John Piper, J. I. Packer, Chuck Colson, Ravi Zacharias, Tim Keller, Al Mohler, and Mark Driscoll."[15] Canadian Baptist Michael Haykin, who teaches at the Southern Baptist Theological Seminary, has beckoned his colleagues to a much more traditional understanding of the sacraments.[16] The Institute of Reformed Baptist Studies, which has now become the International Reformed Baptist Seminary, has encouraged a more confessional, liturgical, and catholic way of inculcating Baptist faith today.[17] An increasing number of Baptists are even using Aquinas in their catechetical work.[18] Of course, in free-church fashion, these men reserve the right to disagree with even the best-known doctors of the church, not to mention each other. But a bevy of other, even-more-catholic free-church thinkers like Derek C. Hatch of Howard Payne University have called their readers to pursue *"ressourcement,"* a courageous development among those whose churches are among the last redoubts of anti-Catholicism.[19] All of these churchmen champion freedom of conscience. The Bible by itself, they avow, should norm our teaching. They are doing what

also Harmon, *Baptists, Catholics, and the Whole Church: Partners in the Pilgrimage to Unity* (Hyde Park, NY: New City, 2021).

14. Malcolm B. Yarnell III, *The Formation of Christian Doctrine* (Nashville: B&H Academic, 2007), 180.

15. Gregg R. Allison, *Historical Theology: An Introduction to Christian Doctrine* (Grand Rapids: Zondervan, 2011), 11.

16. Michael A. G. Haykin, *Amidst Us Our Belovèd Stands: Recovering Sacrament in the Baptist Tradition* (Bellingham, WA: Lexham Press, 2022).

17. See their website at https://irbsseminary.org/.

18. See, for example, Daniel W. Houck, *Aquinas, Original Sin, and the Challenge of Evolution* (Cambridge: Cambridge University Press, 2020).

19. Derek C. Hatch, *Thinking with the Church: Toward a Renewal of Baptist Theology*, Free Church, Catholic Tradition (Eugene, OR: Cascade Books, 2018).

they can, though, as free-church Protestants to advocate learning in communion with the saints.

The success of their movement is symbolized visibly in free-church bodies like the Center for Baptist Renewal.[20] Inspired by statesmen like the Baptist Timothy George, an evangelical ecumenist, this center "is a group of orthodox, evangelical Baptists committed to a retrieval of the Great Tradition of the historic church for the renewal of Baptist faith and practice." Two of these Baptists, Lucas Stamps and Matthew Emerson, have raised a new standard of free-church commitment to inculcating Christian faith across time and space. Titled "Evangelical Baptist Catholicity: A Manifesto," it reflects the best in free-church efforts to embrace the great tradition and teach with all the saints. "We encourage a critical but charitable engagement with the whole church of the Lord Jesus Christ, both past and present," its authors declare. "We believe that Baptists have much to contribute as well as much to receive in the great collection of traditions that constitute the holy catholic church. We believe that we are 'traditioned' creatures." Clearly, free-church leaders are sinking much deeper roots in the history of Christian doctrine these days.[21]

Late-Modern Work on the Concept of Tradition

We have seen already that Christians have long disagreed about the ways in which our history ought to shape church teaching. We have also observed that during and after the Enlightenment secular intellectuals and liberal Protestant allies criticized enthrallment to tradition by conservatives, eliciting a backlash of neotraditionalism among some proponents of organic and providential views of development.

20. The center will soon be renamed the David Dockery and Timothy George Center for Baptist Renewal.

21. See the Center's mission statement (https://www.centerforbaptistrenewal.com/about-us) along with R. Lucas Stamps and Matthew Y. Emerson, "Evangelical Baptist Catholicity: A Manifesto," article 5 (https://www.centerforbaptistrenewal.com/evangelical-baptist-catholicity-a-manifesto).

In recent years, moreover, sociologists of knowledge, historians, and students of religion and culture have piggybacked on previous critiques and/or rehabilitations of tradition and analyzed the origins and functions of various traditions in detail. Before I offer my suggestions on the use of tradition in the teaching of the faith in our churches moving forward, I will do well to survey this late-modern scholarship.

The literary scholar Stephen Prickett, a Christian who investigated the ways in which the English Romantics appropriated religion and tradition in their work, can help me paint a broad picture of the late-modern recovery and revision of tradition before I zoom in closely on important recent studies of the origins and social dynamics of (individual) traditions. In *Modernity and the Reinvention of Tradition* (2009), Prickett told a story of the virtual disappearance and subsequent revival of tradition in modernity. "Tradition," he wrote, "as both word and concept, fell . . . far out of use during the seventeenth and eighteenth centuries, and underwent . . . a dramatic revival in the nineteenth and twentieth centuries." Prickett overstated the decline of tradition in the eighteenth century, but this helped him raise a point about the nineteenth-century revival of tradition that informs most work on the subject today: the concept of tradition that was restored for most late-modern, liberal intellectuals differs from the ones I have featured thus far. "For most Enlightenment thinkers," Prickett explained, "the possibility that the kind of knowledge offered by tradition—that is, *any* form of knowledge transmitted from the past—was of sufficient value to command allegiance in itself had to seem remote in the extreme. Tradition, in short, had been what they were fighting against." So when post-Enlightenment liberals appealed to the notion of tradition once again, "it was to create from it something very different from what Augustine, Eusebius, or Cassiodorus would have understood by the word," something nearly "unthinkable" before. They created an understanding of tradition that is more pliable, diverse, and man-made than before, less divine and determinative of everyday behavior than the notions of tradition I have featured in this volume.[22]

The benchmark studies of tradition and traditions in the last several decades have taken this narrative largely for granted. Edward Shils, for example, a sociologist who worked at the University of Chicago, wrote a landmark work titled *Tradition* (1981) that was referred to by most later writers on the subject and evinced a late-modern perspective on tradition "unthinkable" (or rare) before the eighteenth century. "The givenness of a tradition is more problematic than it looks," Shils said in what by then came close to a truism. "Every tradition, however broad or narrow, offers a possibility of a variety of responses. Every tradition, given though it is, opens potentialities for a diversity of responses." Some moderns, of course, still chafe at traditions as confining and oppressive—but this is naïve. All that is has a past, and all novelty results from engagement with the past. Nearly all traditions change, and most change is supported by traditional materials. "A tradition," Shils allowed, "a particular interpretation or a mode of interpreting a sacred text, a particular style of painting or a particular form of the novel—once established and authoritatively presented might become a fairly long-lasting possession." Nevertheless, "in those categories of human activities which attract persons of strong intelligence and imagination, it is not likely to be held very long in the exact pattern in which it was received." Traditions no longer need hem people in. They are clearly social constructs—even if ordained by the gods, or by God. They give meaning and direction to everyday practice but do so as life-giving sources of inspiration more than stultifying bulwarks of belief and behavior.[23]

The book on traditions best known by nonspecialists underscores this late-modern angle on their origins, makeup, and functions. *The Invention of Tradition* (1983), coedited most famously by lifelong Marxist historian Eric Hobsbawm (University of London), explored

22. Stephen Prickett, *Modernity and the Reinvention of Tradition: Backing into the Future* (Cambridge: Cambridge University Press, 2009), vii, 33, 189.

23. Edward Shils, *Tradition* (Chicago: University of Chicago Press, 1981), 44–45.

many novel, quite modern traditions invented with an ersatz air of antiquity—the highland tradition of Scotland, rituals performed by and for the British monarchs, traditions that shape the common life of universities—the list goes on and on. In "Inventing Traditions," the book's introduction, Hobsbawm interpreted these rites as modern substitutes for no-longer-credible ancient traditions. The latter, many of which were maintained in churches, had arisen from religious and cultural norms that were now obsolete (at least in Hobsbawm's view). But the former, despite being dressed up as ancient, proved no less novel for their pomp and circumstance. Further, he granted, "it seems clear that, in spite of much invention, new traditions have not filled more than a small part of the space left by the secular decline of both old tradition and custom; as might be expected in societies in which the past becomes increasingly less relevant as a model or precedent for most forms of human behavior." Hobsbawm's traditions were flimsy constructions, despite all their gilding and ornate pageantry. They soothed and inspired those who still held them dear. But they symbolized a yearning for substance and profundity, meaning and direction, that materialists (like Hobsbawm) make difficult to find.[24]

Many theologians now working on tradition have embraced these claims about its social construction and cultural utility and used them to argue for a new kind of critical engagement with the past. Not many of them have said things that help people teaching in conservative, confessional ecclesiastical settings. But at least they have treated our traditions with respect, inventing new ways to make use of historic Christian doctrines, symbols, rituals, and forms. About a decade after the publications of Shils and Hobsbawm, Delwin Brown of the Iliff School of Theology, for instance, invited liberal colleagues to "return to traditions. Not, of course," he said, "to traditions as they were understood by the Enlightenment mentality that uncritically dismissed them or by the counter-Enlightenment mind that uncritically embraced

---

24. Eric Hobsbawm and Terence Ranger, eds., *The Invention of Tradition*, Past and Present Publications (Cambridge: Cambridge University Press, 1983), 11.

them, but to traditions as they persistently show themselves to be—dynamic and diverse streams of being and meaning that mold and are molded, continue and create, save and destroy." Theology "should be the critical analyst and creative conveyor of the vast conceptual resource, actual and potential, of religious traditions," Brown suggested. "In thus critically and creatively reconstructing the past, a theology is a tradition's caregiver."[25]

David Brown (no relation), who lectured in Durham and later St. Andrews, repeated this refrain, going so far as to suggest that constructions of tradition over the course of church history sometimes achieve a kind of revelatory quality equal to that of the Scriptures. "Changes in our conception of how the Bible came to be written and in the nature of its impact in subsequent centuries," Brown made bold to say, "require a different conception of the relation between revelation and tradition than that which has held sway throughout the history of Christianity. So far from thinking of the Bible as the already fully painted canvas and the traditions of the later Church as offering at most some optional extra colouring, we need to think of a continuous dynamic of tradition operating both within the Bible and beyond. That 'beyond,'" he underlined, "will then sometimes be found to merit status as revelation no less clear than what preceded it."[26]

Michel Despland of Université Concordia Montréal pointed out that late-modern understandings of tradition had political implications. "Most contemporary authors promoting 'tradition,'" he vented prophetically, "pursue a sort of utopian dream; they tend to see tradition as issuing in a perfectly transparent and egalitarian community, where no one rules over any one else, since 'tradition' rules. They try to save themselves the trouble of being political." But if traditions are constructed for man-made ends, Despland went on, those who make them are, perforce, engaging in politics and ought to proceed

---

25. Delwin Brown, *Boundaries of Our Habitations: Tradition and Theological Construction*, SUNY Series in Religious Studies (Albany: State University of New York Press, 1994), 137–38.

26. David Brown, *Tradition and Imagination: Revelation and Change* (Oxford: Oxford University Press, 1999), 365.

with a commitment to justice. Kathryn Tanner of Yale inferred, consequently, that the Christian tradition is now best understood as a history of argument within the body of Christ. It should not be seen as "a process of transmission, since there is no already unified body of stuff to be transmitted and the materials at issue include ones supplied by one's contemporaries. Instead of a process of transmission," Tanner concluded, "tradition amounts to a process of argument, among upholders of different Christian viewpoints, whether in the past or present. Or, one might say, what is now transmitted is the practice of argument itself."[27]

A few theologians at work on tradition in a late-modern mode have raised concerns that bear directly on the project of composing and making good use of a *global* history of doctrine. The Cuban-American Catholic Orlando Espín spoke for many with his calls for a global perspective on the question of tradition. Too often, he confirmed, academics assume that the Christian tradition is the Western Christian tradition—and this, of course, must change.[28] And the American Baptist leader Dale Irvin wrote a book on the Christian tradition whose main contribution is to affirm that Christianity has always been diverse (à la Espín and others) but to show that its diversity is not absolute. "Often it is assumed that the notion of a tradition implies continuity," Irvin explained, "or that it has a fundamental *identity with itself* over time. But historical changes introduce differences into a tradition, giving rise to its *non-identity with itself*. Religious traditions in particular are not the static monoliths their defenders often claim

---

27. Michel Despland, "Tradition," in *Historicizing 'Tradition' in the Study of Religion*, ed. Steven Engler and Gregory P. Grieve, Religion and Society (Berlin: de Gruyter, 2005), 29; Kathryn Tanner, "Tradition and Theological Judgment in Light of Postmodern Cultural Criticism," in *Tradition and Tradition Theories: An International Discussion*, ed. Thorsten Larbig and Siegfried Wiedenhofer (Berlin: LIT, 2006), 244–45. For similar perspectives from elsewhere on the planet, see Barbara Schoppelreich and Siegfried Wiedenhofer, eds., *Zur Logik religiöser Traditionen* (Frankfurt: IKO – Verlag für Interkulturelle Kommunikation, 1998); Marcel Sarot and Gijsbert van den Brink, eds., *Identity and Change in the Christian Tradition* (Frankfurt: Lang, 1999).

28. Orlando O. Espín, "Toward the Construction of an Intercultural Theology of (Catholic) Tradition," in Larbig and Wiedenhofer, *Tradition and Tradition Theories*, 281–319.

them to be, but are heterogeneous and multivocal arenas of contention and change. Composed of multiple voices that are different, and often in considerable disagreement with one another, they are pluralized internally." So far so good, at least to most late-moderns, but this does not render the Christian tradition incoherent. The history of our faith is like a rhizome, he said. It is a nonlinear network in which its varied nodes are nonetheless joined together. It is clearly diverse, but it is united as well. And "if we must confront the repressive character of totalized history or absolutized tradition," he noted in the affirmative, "it seems to me that at the same time we must avoid the error of absolutizing difference itself." Our tradition's "alterity," its "otherness," he wrote, "is not an absolute difference but a differentiation. The difference of a tradition is difference-in-relation."[29] Andrew Walls, Lamin Sanneh, and the other church historians and missiologists represented in chapter 2 have said much the same thing.

There is much to ponder here, particularly for those who want to teach in the churches across time and space. Inasmuch as these late-modern views of tradition make claims about our faith, and claims about the ways in which we hand on the faith, traditional believers must meet them head-on. We will see in what follows that the present writer holds to a view of tradition more spiritual, catholic, and even providential than the views just presented (in the paragraphs above). But he also affirms an understanding of the faith more global and diverse than the ones most common in medieval and early modern European history—an understanding informed by a wide range of late-modern, postcolonial friends. Is it possible to maintain a classical perspective on the nature of the church while embracing a late-modern view of its diversity? How can teachers hand on the faith once delivered in catechesis shaped by the history of doctrine while paying due attention to non-Western Christian voices? I will answer these questions in the section to come.

29. Dale T. Irvin, *Christian Histories, Christian Traditioning: Rendering Accounts* (Maryknoll, NY: Orbis Books, 1998), 46–47, 142.

Thinking in, with, and under the Christian Church

One of the most important lessons we can learn from the study of the global history of doctrine is to shed pedagogical parochialism by outgrowing it. Blinkered perspectives on the beauty and benefits of Christian faith and practice throughout church history, and on the burdens and blight of "Christianity" as proffered by the most selfish members of the worldwide family of God, can impoverish and distort our identity as Christians and prospects as followers of Jesus. They can make us narrow-minded, keeping us from understanding God, the Bible, the nature of our faith, and its practice at large in a comprehensive manner. They can also stunt our witness and everyday discipleship, keeping us from living out our faith in the world, loving God and our neighbors, as the Lord has commanded. No one will ever gain a God's-eye view of the global history of doctrine. We all have our limits. But the more we try to grow in our knowledge of the faith of the whole people of God, the better we will be at helping others to flourish in and with—indeed under the nurture and admonition of—the holy catholic church.

C. S. Lewis wrote an argument for reading old books that applies to the teaching of the global history of doctrine. "Every age has its own outlook," Lewis suggested by way of introduction to a reprint of *De Incarnatione Verbi Dei* (ca. 335), Athanasius of Alexandria's best-known treatise.

> It is specially good at seeing certain truths and specially liable to make certain mistakes. We all, therefore, need the books that will correct the characteristic mistakes of our own period. And that means the old books. . . . Not, of course, that there is any magic about the past. People were no cleverer then than they are now; they made as many mistakes as we. But not the *same* mistakes. They will not flatter us in the errors we are already committing; and their own errors, being now open and palpable, will not endanger us. Two heads are better than

one, not because either is infallible, but because they are unlikely to go wrong in the same direction.[30]

This logic also pertains to learning from believers in other parts of the world. They are no smarter than we. They commit as many errors. But their angles of vision and cultural experiences can complement ours. We need such kindred to expand, fill out, and color in our perceptions of the Lord and his will.

Georges Florovsky made a similar point on the existential value of the ancient church fathers. "I have often a strange feeling," Florovsky confessed.

When I read the ancient classics of Christian theology, the fathers of the church, I find them more relevant to the troubles and problems of my own time than the production of modern theologians. The fathers were wrestling with existential problems, with those revelations of the eternal issues which were described and recorded in Holy Scripture. I would risk a suggestion that St. Athanasius and St. Augustine are much more up to date than many of our theological contemporaries. The reason is very simple: they were dealing with things and not with the maps, they were concerned not so much with what man can believe as with what God had done for man. We have, "in a time such as this," to enlarge our perspective, to acknowledge the masters of old, and to attempt for our own age an existential synthesis of Christian experience.[31]

The same logic applies to our cross-cultural reading, listening, and learning. Very often, our kindred in faraway environments live out the faith in a manner unhampered by our own academic, political, cultural, and peer-group obsessions. They can help us break free of

30. C. S. Lewis, introduction to *The Incarnation of the Word of God, Being the Treatise of St. Athanasius "De Incarnatione Verbi Dei,"* trans. by an anon. religious of C.S.M.V. S. (New York: Macmillan, 1946), 6–7.

31. Georges Florovsky, *Bible, Church, Tradition: An Eastern Orthodox View,* in *The Collected Works of Georges Florovsky* (Belmont, MA: Nordland, 1972), 1:16.

our hermeneutical ruts and pedagogical routines and see the main things clearly and directly once again.

We fail to listen to them well, though, when doing so primarily for reasons of our own, when distracted by our own thoughts, needs, or agendas. We fail to honor their concerns when we cut them into sound bites, fragments, or units, abstract them from the history, language, and culture in which they took shape, or appropriate essentialized views of their meanings to suit our own ends. We learn best from other people when we listen to them patiently, interpret their actions in ways they would affirm, and resist the temptation to colonize their work. There is no such thing as absolute objectivity. We engage other people from our own points of view and make good on what we learn in our own social contexts. There are better and worse ways, though, to render and profit from other people's teaching. The best ways, moreover, treat their teaching with respect, recounting their concerns on behalf and for the sake of the whole people of God.

Some modern theologians treat the Christian tradition like a big-box store. They enter it sporadically to meet their own needs, push a cart through its aisles with a shopping list in hand, and select those items that assist them with assignments they have underway. Nearly everything they purchase originated in settings of which they know little. It was grown or manufactured in other times and places, packaged by people most often unknown, and shipped by distributors in business for profit. This creates a vast distance between these theologians and the sources of the doctrines conveyed to their students, rendering unstable their connections to others in the worldwide body of Christ. In a day and age when farm-to-table eating is in vogue, this pedagogical method is ironic, tragic, and often even harmful.

To mix our metaphors a bit, much modern theology is like cherry pie. It is made by bakers who travel in regions marked out in advance for the features of the fruit that their trees are known to yield. They select choice cherries from several different orchards, favoring the ones for which their recipes call. They devote little energy to individual groves. They do not care much about the history of the trees, the soil in which they grow, or the work of the farmers who bring them to fruition. Their aim is not to help others understand cherries in all of their variety, their natural evolution, or the reasons why people prefer different kinds. Their aim, to be sure, is to make their own pies, improving on the flavors and textures of others.

These are not good ways to teach the faith of the church. They engender competition among our instructors and consumeristic treatment of the voices of others in the Christian tradition. They foster parochialism—not, of course, the kind that derives from triumphalistic views of the glories of our own denominations, but an even worse kind: that which values the genius of individual teachers over the witness of the church through the ages. God's people do not need individual retrievals of fragments, or units, or cherries from the past. We need the whole feast of faith: the Scriptures primarily, but creeds, confessions, and traditions as well, interpreted with help from the whole family of God. We want our most faithful, learned, and diligent instructors to serve us this feast. We do not want scholars, though, altering the menu with their latest inventions, or suggesting to students that their own idiosyncrasies are worth as much attention as the holy catholic faith. We need faithful, humble, ecclesial theologians to lead God's people to maturity in Christ, not self-interested, aspiring, academic virtuosos who upstage the faith God has given to the church.

My concern about the narrowness of much of our instruction is like that of Lewis Ayres regarding recent work on the doctrine of the Trinity in ancient Christianity. In Ayres's estimation, our modern engagement with Nicene faith is most often superficial. It quickly abstracts and arranges ideal types from the writings of the fathers. Then it renders those types in an ahistorical manner, restricting the scope of the sources retrieved—not to mention their potential to speak to us today. Or in Ayres's own words, the methods employed "obstruct dense engagement with pro-Nicene theology by hiding the need for a dialogue between significantly distinct theological cultures and the possibility of considering pro-Nicene arguments in detail as sentences that may still be spoken today." In much recent teaching, both "history and authority in theology are reconfigured in the direction of modernity's necessary reworking of the pre-modern."[32] The result, all too often, is a loss in our capacity to think with the ancients and connect organically—through history, geography, and cultural distinctions— with people from the past.

My interest in expanding our pedagogical purview resembles the interest of T. S. Eliot in the proper relation of the poet to tradition. A great poet, he said, "can neither take the past as a lump, an indiscriminate bolus, nor can he form himself wholly on one or two private admirations, nor can he form himself wholly upon one preferred period. The first course is inadmissible, the second is an important experience of youth, and the third is a pleasant and highly desirable supplement. The poet must be very conscious of the main current, which does not at all flow invariably through the most distinguished reputations."[33] Great teachers of the church, like literary artists, must outgrow the limits of an immature parochialism. They should think, speak, and write with a real sense of history, a fulsome connection to the most important currents of the theological past—whether or not they have flowed through the work of famous people.

Parochialism appears in many different guises, some of which are worn inadvertently by teachers who are liberating students from mistakes and abuses committed by others from across time and space. And this brings us back to Walls and his call to combine the "indigenizing principle" of Christian instruction and its twin, the "pilgrim principle"[34]—surmounting *all* obstacles to Christian communion: ethnocentric, presentist, and individualistic. The indigenizing principle

32. Lewis Ayres, *Nicaea and Its Legacy: An Approach to Fourth-Century Trinitarian Theology* (Oxford: Oxford University Press, 2004), 384–429 (quotation from 392).

33. T. S. Eliot, "Tradition and the Individual Talent," in *The Sacred Wood and Major Early Essays* (Mineola, NY: Dover, 1998; orig. 1920), 29.

34. Andrew F. Walls, "The Gospel as Prisoner and Liberator of Culture," in Walls, *The Missionary Movement in Christian History*, 8–9.

suggests that Christianity is always apprehended in diverse cultural forms or patterns that should shape our transmission of the gospel. The pilgrim principle suggests, on the other hand, that all Christianity is universal too. We do not learn from others by exploiting their productions for self-serving reasons, taking them out of context. But neither do we grow, or honor other people, by engaging their cultures in a patronizing manner, as though they lack the strength to accommodate communion with the rest of God's family. Many now assume that our cultures are inviolable and teach Christian faith in a nondoctrinal way, as a thin story of Jesus and his care for the weak. This helps them fit their teaching into any cultural package. But it bankrupts recipients. The real Christian faith makes claims upon our lives, claims best explained with the whole counsel of God—not the whole counsel of God as imparted in the West, but the whole counsel of God as conveyed by the whole people of God, past and present. Indigenous believers in every time and place need the spiritual nutrition provided by teachers who serve them unstintingly from the Lord's banquet.

So how can we teach in a less parochial manner? What should we offer to the people in our care? And how can we do so without transgressing our denominational rules, confessional commitments, and cultural priorities? Perhaps just as importantly, how can we do so with proper humility? No one is omniscient except the Lord himself. We all have limits. We also have preferences, some of which are used by the Lord for our good and the blessing of others in the global family of God. So how are we to serve as both loyal representatives of our own communities and faithful instructors of the universal church? A great deal of prayer and labor in the Scriptures and church history is required. There are also some pedagogical pointers to consider.

The most promising approach to teaching in, with, and under the global church of God is *evangelical* and *catholic*: eager to present the good news of Jesus Christ with cultural ductility but careful to offer the entire feast of faith in accordance with the best of the Christian tradition. It assumes that the teaching of our churches develops, sometimes for the better, on the basis of the Word as interpreted with excellence by authorized teachers in light of new learning, hermeneutical refinements, and cultural interaction among God's people (our churches, of course, appointing authorized teachers in somewhat different ways). Even the most conservative Orthodox teachers of the faith say their doctrines developed in early church history. Even old school Protestants affirm that their teaching on Scripture and salvation underwent some refinement in the sixteenth century. Many of us today include concern for the poor in our congregational ministries, teaching it in terms specified in the global south in the mid-twentieth century. I affirm these kinds of development wholeheartedly. They are evidence that Christians do learn from one another across time and space, expanding the horizons of their pedagogical ministries. But evangelical-catholics, at least those most devoted to the faith of the church, give orthodox teaching—the faith that they receive from duly authorized teachers—the benefit of the doubt until very strong majorities of ecclesiastical leaders from many different cultures discern that the Lord wants their teaching to improve. They move past parochialism not by revising their instruction all the time, in every new social and cultural situation, or as advocated by coteries of academic leaders, but by steady conversation among church officials on how to respond well to new information, historical developments, and global perspectives on Scripture and tradition.

To put this another way, evangelical-catholics endeavor to transmit as much traditional teaching as the Scriptures allow—the Scriptures, that is, as interpreted not by individual scholars but by the church at large. We have seen already that the worldwide church has not always agreed on the contours of faith. At this point in history, though, most of the mainstream, orthodox churches agree about most of the church's basic doctrines (if not about the best ways to teach their details): God and the Trinity, the person and work of Christ, salvation by grace, the authority of Scripture. Where we disagree, moreover, we do so on the basis of established traditions of doctrinal divergence; the differences that matter to Christians who mean it are encoded in centuries-old catechetical tools. In practice, then, the most helpful evangelical-catholics hold the first four ecumenical councils as sacrosanct (because thoughtful Christians have for fifteen hundred years agreed that they convey their content correctly, reliably, and savingly). They view their own confessions as largely-though-not-altogether unchangeable (because their officials have for centuries agreed that they teach the best system of belief on offer). And they treat the remainder of the catholic tradition with the utmost respect (whether or not they rejoice in all of its details). They place a heavy burden of proof on those calling for revision. Their instincts are traditional. They affirm, once again, that our teaching can develop—and has in fact developed through the history of the church. Our doctrine can advance on the basis of the Bible, but only as our leaders from all around the world see a need for advancement.[35]

An evangelical-catholic approach to the faith does not solve all the problems addressed in this book. Nor does it secure the kind of doctrinal stability that many people want—or doctrinal diversity that other people want. The power and privilege of educated, enfranchised, Westerners, especially, have raised grave doubts about the promise of an evangelical-catholic catechesis. History shows that Western might militates against multiethnic conversation. Still, an honest and open evangelical-catholicism—aided by ongoing, straightforward efforts to redress the balance of power in the global family of God—offers the wisest, most faithful, and inclusive way forward for those who want to teach in, with, and under the church.

35. I should clarify here that some who have called themselves evangelical-catholics have proven less catholic than I would have wished, advocating rather more idiosyncratic teachings on a few key doctrines than most catholics do: Philip Schaff, for example, whose peculiar, evolutionary view of Christian faith is sketched briefly above (in chapters 1 and 3), and Robert Jenson, who leveled strong criticism of most catholic christological teaching (to take one example from his pedagogical ministry), but who went on to found, with his friend Carl Braaten, the Center for Catholic and Evangelical Theology, whose journal *Pro Ecclesia* is full of the kind of traditional instruction being advocated here (https://www.pro-ecclesia.org/). We could point to more examples of such inconsistency. Most, however, are found in instructors with deeply catholic instincts whose evangelical faith has simply led to proposals for doctrinal development.

This style of catechesis is clarified further by comparison with other leading ways of using history to hand on the faith, especially those treated at the top of this chapter. An evangelical-catholic engagement with the past will differ from the way of *constructive theology* mainly in its attitude toward the tradition as channeled through the history of the church and its ministries. It trusts in the redeeming work of God through history—and trusts in the providential purposes of God with respect to redemption, purposes that center on the church and its teaching. Despite the awful sins of believers through the ages, despite the many ways in which the faith has been weaponized to subjugate others, evangelical-catholics confess that "in Christ" God is "reconciling the world to himself" and, what is more, reconciling the members of his body to each other (2 Cor. 5:19; Eph. 2:11–22). They affirm that the saints are "ambassadors for Christ," assigned to "the ministry of reconciliation" (2 Cor. 5:20, 18). And they know that the church is not subject to decay. "The gates of Hades," Jesus said, "will not prevail against it" (Matt. 16:18). So they treat the tradition with a chastened respect, not deaf to the cries of those damaged by Christians but certain that the Lord "will bring every deed to judgement" (Eccles. 12:14) and that "all things work together for good for those who love God" (Rom. 8:28), those who partake in the mission of the Lord. They even grant church authorities a chastened respect, not following their counsel with blind veneration but viewing them as shepherds who are now "keeping watch" and will later "give an account" of their work before God (Heb. 13:17). They do not seek to deconstruct the history of the church and its structures of authority. They do not try to reconstruct their own, more liberating concepts of God and God's work in the world. They labor as adherents to the holy catholic church, relying on the history of the Lord's saving work and their leaders' best efforts to interpret that work as they hand on the faith, fight against evil, and pursue God's justice in the world.

An evangelical-catholic approach to the past will differ from the way of *retrieval theology* in the range of church history engaged by teachers and the authority assigned, in the formulation of doctrine, to the leaders of the church as compared to independent theologians (or groups of theologians). Retrieval theologians collect small fragments or units from the past and deploy them in support of their own "constructive moves" (theological improvements). Evangelical-catholics embrace the whole faith as received from their elders and pass it on to others in keeping with tradition as informed by church leaders from all around the world. For retrieval theologians, the main event in teaching is one's own contribution to contemporary discourse. For evangelical-catholics, the main event in teaching is transmission of the faith in an ecumenical way. Retrieval theology is done in the schools (at least in the main). It prepares young scholars to become theologians. Evangelical-catholic work occurs in the church (at least in the main). It prepares lay Christians for the love of God and neighbor. It provokes "one another to love and good deeds" (Heb. 10:24).

The differences between evangelical-catholicism and *ressourcement* have primarily to do with the circumscribed nature of and sources explored in most *ressourcement*. Evangelical-catholic teaching is capacious in scope. It inculcates students with a comprehensive faith from the Scriptures and most of the Christian tradition. *Ressourcement* is rather more confined. It started as an effort to escape what proponents called the arid scholasticism of modern Catholic manuals of orthodox dogma by mining the writings of the early church fathers and looking most closely at their spiritual theology. The aim was to energize Roman Catholic teaching and speak to the hearts and minds of modern Europeans (and others, of course). In time it would grow and become more expansive, emphasizing writings from a wide array of sources (Scripture, liturgy, creeds, and church councils in addition to the work of more premodern writers). Even then, though, its purpose was to fuel a reform of modern Roman Catholic thinking and revitalize Catholic spirituality.

Evangelical-catholicism differs from the way of most *free-church theologies* by placing more weight on the creeds and confessions and granting more authority to churchwide leaders when exegeting Scripture and handing on the faith. Most free-church teachers have no creed but the Bible. Evangelical-catholics use creeds, confessions, and the history of doctrine to interpret the Bible. Free-church leaders are fiercely independent; they refuse to align their pedagogical priorities with rules constructed by external authorities. Evangelical-catholics are much more communal; they teach church doctrine in keeping with the saints, submitting their instruction to guidelines received from the Christian tradition. They embrace church history in a more fulsome manner. They interpret God's Word and make sense of God's will in concert with Christians across time and space.

It should go without saying now that evangelical-catholics hold a view of *tradition* that differs somewhat from those of many late-moderns at work in the academy. They agree that most traditions are socially constructed and hence more pliable than many used to think. They concur that church history is much more diverse than even the most traveled premodern figures understood. Nevertheless, they affirm with their ancient Christian kin that tradition, *paradosis* (παράδοσις), handing on the faith, is commanded by the Lord, who promised to be with us and guide us as we go. What is more, they affirm that *some* of their traditions have come from the Lord. As Jesus told the Twelve, "When the Spirit of truth comes, he will guide you into all the truth; for he will not speak on his own, but will speak whatever he hears, and he will declare to you the things that are to come. He will glorify me, because he will take what is mine and declare it to you. All that the Father has is mine. For this reason I said that he will take what is mine and declare it to you" (John 16:13–15). The apostles believed that the Spirit had told them what to hand on to others—and this is why they took their stewardship so seriously. "Guard the good treasure entrusted to you, with the help of the Holy Spirit," Paul urged Timothy (2 Tim. 1:14). "And what you have heard from me . . . entrust to faithful people who will be able to teach others" (2:2). "Stand firm and hold fast to the traditions that you were taught by us, either by word of mouth or by our letter," he wrote (2 Thess. 2:15). "I commend you because you . . . maintain the traditions just as I handed them on to you" (1 Cor. 11:2). Evangelical-catholics understand that tradition has often been oppressive. They confess that their forebears often used tradition to marginalize others—and they grieve this deeply. But the answer to this failure, they dare to profess, is not social construction or greater independence but a far more catholic understanding of tradition—one that sheds its parochialism and outgrows its sins by learning from a wider range of saints around the world.

Evangelical-catholics begin where we are, using our own churches' teaching tools, following the rules laid out by our leaders, and honoring our people's cultural inclinations. We are creedal, confessional, loyal to our tribes. We do what we can, though, to broaden their horizons and teach toward a more universal Christian faith. We do not leave our people unsure of who they are or what our churches hold dear. We pay due heed to the indigenizing principle. But neither do we leave them in their own little worlds. We serve them as much of the feast of faith as possible. We use the history of doctrine to deepen their connection to the whole body of Christ, the entire family of God. And we teach in such a way as to "equip the saints" for ministry,

> building up the body of Christ, until all of us come to the unity of the faith and of the knowledge of the Son of God, to maturity, to the measure of the full stature of Christ. We must no longer be children, tossed to and fro and blown about by every wind of doctrine, by people's trickery, by their craftiness in deceitful scheming. But speaking the truth in love, we must grow up in every way into him who is the head, into Christ, from whom the whole body, joined and knitted together by every ligament with which it is equipped, as each part is working properly, promotes the body's growth in building itself up in love. (Eph. 4:12–16)

These are ancient admonitions, cherished for ages as a spur to discipleship. If there ever was a time, though, to put them into practice, overcoming narrowness, chauvinism, and ignorance within the body of Christ, it is now.

Conclusion

We declare to you what was from the beginning, what we have heard, what we have seen with our eyes, what we have looked at and touched with our hands, concerning the word of life—this life was revealed, and we have seen it and testify to it, and declare to you the eternal life that was with the Father and was revealed to us—we declare to you what we have seen and heard so that you also may have fellowship with us; and truly our fellowship is with the Father and with his Son Jesus Christ. We are writing these things so that our joy may be complete.

—1 John 1:1–4

One of the most important writers in my own nation's history is the Concord Transcendentalist Ralph Waldo Emerson, who flourished at the time in which America's cultural propensities were formed and its Christians began to send missionaries abroad in unprecedented numbers. In a spate of famous speeches and best-selling essays, Emerson encouraged us to trust in ourselves. Though the apostle Paul had long ago admonished the Philippians, "Do nothing from selfish ambition or conceit, but in humility regard others as better than yourselves" (Phil. 2:3), Emerson insisted in his essay "Self-Reliance" (1841) that "to believe your *own* thought, to believe that what is true for you in your private heart is true for all men—that is genius. Speak your latent conviction," he exhorted tens of thousands,

> and it shall be the universal sense; for the inmost in due time becomes the outmost, and our first thought is rendered back to us by the trumpets of the Last Judgment. Familiar as the voice of the mind is to each, the highest merit we ascribe to Moses, Plato and Milton is that they set at naught books and traditions, and spoke not what men, but what *they* thought. A man should learn to detect and watch that gleam of light which flashes across his mind from within, more than the lustre of the firmament of bards and sages.[1]

So much for humble regard for the contributions of others. So much for church history and catholicity. Emerson and many other modern Western writers have admonished eager listeners to leave the past behind and blaze their own, new trails: "[If] a man claims to know and speak of God and carries you backward to the phraseology of some old mouldered nation in another country, in another world, believe him not. Is the acorn better than the oak which is its fulness and completion? Is the parent better than the child into whom he has cast his ripened being? Whence then this worship of the past? The centuries are conspirators against the sanity and authority of the soul."[2]

This fountainhead of US American ambition, of Western liberal hubris exported overseas, of late modern, independent, critical engagement, has inspired countless millions to eschew the dead hand of convention and conformity and muster the courage to pursue their own ideals.

Though enticing to those who have been hobbled by history, oppressed by convention, or silenced by tradition, this is not a good way to hand the faith on to others. It militates against such *paradosis*

1. Ralph Waldo Emerson, "Self-Reliance," in *The Selected Writings of Ralph Waldo Emerson*, ed. Brooks Atkinson (New York: Modern Library, 1992), 132.
2. Emerson, "Self-Reliance," 142.

(παράδοσις), in fact. As I have tried to suggest in this prefatory volume, narrowminded views of the Christian tradition, blinkered perspectives on the faith once delivered, proudly parochial approaches to discipleship are not best countered by yet more individualism, ignorance, or chauvinism. Parochialism is stemmed best within our congregations by instructors who can teach across both time and space. Good teachers know better than to educate others with their own views alone—even if those views are based upon the Word of God. They know it takes the whole family of God to raise saints to maturity in Christ. They know this work is too important to undertake in isolation from their siblings in the Lord's global family, without access to the riches of the whole feast of faith.

Let us never give up on the God-given lessons of the lives and the loves of our own closest kin. But neither let us shirk those aspects of the faith that our own, dearest relatives do not know well. If the church is really one, holy, catholic, and apostolic, if its citizens hail from every tribe, tongue, and nation, then our teaching must account for the faith, devotion, and biblical engagement of believers everywhere—no matter how far away they are in time, geography, or cultural location. This requires new learning on the part of all instructors. It requires real knowledge of the global history of doctrine. And it leads, when done well, to authentic communion with the whole body of Christ and, thereby, "with the Father and . . . his Son Jesus Christ." Let us teach in this way—let us go to this trouble—that the "joy" of the whole family of God "may be complete" (1 John 1:3–4).

Index